MAKE MONEY
with the New Tax Laws

MAKE MONEY
with the New Tax Laws

Andrew Leckey

Bonus Books, Chicago

91   90   89   88   87   5   4   3   2   1

Library of Congress Catalog Card Number: 86-72777

ISBN: 0-933893-32-9 (paperbound) 0-933893-26-4 (clothbound)

Bonus Books, Inc.
160 East Illinois Street
Chicago, Illinois 60611

Printed in the United States of America

To the memory of
Ellen Leckey

Contents

Acknowledgments

A number of top-flight professionals helped make this book possible. Special thanks to Robert S. Greisman, partner in the Grant Thornton accounting firm, for his advice and analysis of content, and to Coleen V. Marren for her organizational skill and research assistance throughout the entire project. Richard A. Helfand, partner, and Ronald S. Sonenthal, senior tax consultant, of the Arthur Andersen accounting firm provided family tax data for Chapter 12. Financial advice in that chapter was formulated with the help of Charles B. Lefkowitz, chairman of the International Association for Financial Planning; Glenn K. Gabbard, director of the financial consultant support center of Shearson Lehman Brothers; and Marilyn R. Capelli, president of Forest Financial Advisors. James H. Schlesser, partner in the Touche Ross accounting firm, assisted in answering the most-asked tax questions in Chapter 15. Anne Moore also helped with research.

1   Make Money

Make money. That's the bottom line for American investors with the new tax laws. Finding the best strategy to cope with a new investment world of lower tax brackets and fewer shelters has sent everyone from Wall Street to Main Street scurrying.

Brokerage firms are pushing high-yield choices and variations on one shelter that was mercifully spared, the tax-exempt municipal bond. Banks are trotting out advertising campaigns to let investors know the IRA isn't really dead. Financial planners are shifting clients out of traditional partnerships that functioned as tax shelters. Bond houses are getting ready for the return of many investors to fixed-rate investments. Since the home remains one of the few tax breaks still around, everyone from real estate brokers to lenders pitching home equity loans is trying to figure all the angles.

Long before the new tax laws were signed by President Reagan in what he termed the World Series of tax reform, the word "simplification" was dropped from the title. Good thing, too. Eighteen-hundred pages is definitely not simple.

But, complex as it all may appear, you can make money with the new tax laws. They're part of a dramatic new investment climate in which instruments are packaged in fancy names and wrappers, with fees often slapped on when you're not looking. More than a few investments are designed to look as though they were specifically designed to cope with the new tax laws, but not all of them may be right for you. Making money requires understanding all the variables, selecting the right group of investments for your particular situation at each stage of your life, and being patient enough to wait for solid long-term results.

The opportunities to make money aren't just for big-buck folks who got theirs the "old-fashioned way," by inheriting it. Many highly profitable mutual funds require small minimum investments or, in some cases, set no minimums at all. The basics of making money are no different whether you're a small investor scrimping to put aside a few extra dollars, or an executive aiming to be fat and sassy in retirement one day. People who earn the most money, after all, are not necessarily the people who wind up with the most money.

When Rep. Dan Rostenkowski (D-Ill.) and Sen. Bob Packwood (R-Ore.) came down from the mountain with the tablets of reform, they considered Americans to have been kicking up their heels for decades in a "lurid" lifestyle of consumer debt and tax schemes. Once the White House signed off on this new morality of personal finance, it was a fresh start. (Not that a mounting federal deficit might not send them scampering back up that mountain again for revisions that might even include hikes in tax brackets, mind you, but that's not something to worry about right now.)

To begin preparing for these sweeping changes that installed the nation's accountants, lawyers and financial planners as spiritual guides, here are the 10 commandments of the new tax laws:

—*Pay off your consumer debt pronto.* The gradual five-year phaseout of the deduction for consumer interest makes carrying around a lot of debt at high interest charges a real burden. Attempt to pay your monthly credit-card bills in a timely fashion too.

—*Don't take anything, such as tax brackets, for granted.* A lot of taxpayers seem to think they're immediately in low tax brackets, but 1987 is a transition period. Even in 1988 a lot of Americans will be in tax brackets higher than that highly-advertised 28 percent. Figure what your actual bracket will be before you make any big personal financial moves.

—*Look into tax-exempt vehicles such as municipal bonds and bond funds, as well as tax-exempt money market funds.* These remain free of federal taxation under the new tax laws. In addition, yields on tax-exempts are currently at historically high levels when compared to taxables. As soon as President Reagan signed the tax bill, big Wall Street investment firms were racing to market with newly-authorized stripped municipal bonds. These are zero-coupon securities one to eight years in maturity designed for investors who are saving for their children's education or for their own retirement. Zero-coupon investments don't pay interest, but are sold at a deep discount. The investor's return comes from the difference between the discounted price and the face value, which he receives at maturity.

—*Consider single-premium whole life insurance policies, which accumulate tax-free and often permit borrowing without interest charges, and single-premium deferred annuities, which are sort of like an IRA with no deduction.* Another deferral tool is the Series EE U.S. savings bond. This still offers a competitive yield despite the fact the Treasury Department lowered the guaranteed minimum on bonds held five years to six percent.

—*Examine high-yield investments, such as high-dividend stocks, high-yield bonds and bond funds and mortgage-backed Ginnie Mae funds in which interest and principal are guaranteed by Uncle Sam.* When tax changes are in full swing, a greater number of Americans will be in lower individual tax brackets, so high yields will make more sense for them. Bonds also look more competitive because stocks no longer enjoy an advantage in capital gains treatment. When looking at individual stocks and mutual funds, remember that some types of companies will be more blessed by the new tax laws than others.

—*Realize how important your home is in financial planning.* Interest on it is still deductible. Furthermore, interest on home equity loans is deductible so long as the amount doesn't exceed the purchase price of the home plus improvements. Many Americans will consolidate their debts into these highly-publicized home equity loans that permit them to borrow based on equity built up over the years. But realize that rates and terms on home equity loans vary considerably among institutions, and that adding additional debt to your home increases your chance of losing it one day.

—*Take advantage of company 401(k) plans.* These tax-deferral vehicles have been cut back to $7,000 annually under the new laws, but are still a worthwhile means of socking money away for retirement. They permit an employee to contribute pretax dollars to a company pool invested in stocks, bonds, or money-market funds, not reported for tax purposes until retirement or severance.

—*Don't automatically reject individual retirement accounts.* For many Americans they'll still be deductible and, for others, it will still be possible to use them as deferral vehicles even without the deduction. Tax-deferred compounding is always worthwhile.

—*Be cautious in considering partnerships.* The goal now is on economic sense, lots of cash and little debt, a reversal of tax shelter philosophies of the past. Also be careful when considering the new shelters designed to have "passive" income to offset present income. Always look closely at the logic behind them. Study the track record of the company offering the shelter.

—*Don't expect children to be the tax shelter they were in the past.* Children's investment income over $1,000 gets taxed in the parents' bracket until age 14. So there will be less emphasis upon high-income investments in the child's name, but instead growth investments such as stock funds and also tax-exempt instruments.

That just scratches the surface, of course. Just figuring out the complex transitional rules is enough to wear out a calculator battery. For 1987, there are five individual tax rates ranging from 11 to 38.5 percent, while in 1988 there are three rates of 15, 28 and 33 percent. Expect your 1987 tax form and new W-4 employee withholding form to be much more difficult.

For someone in a lower tax bracket, the opportunities to save should be better than ever. But "running the numbers" on competing yields at banks and investment firms and structuring the finances required to own a first home are more difficult than ever.

The new tax laws require planning geared more to the individual's circumstances. There are plenty of people just waiting to offer that financial advice—at a price. Don't panic. You can do a lot of your homework yourself and the decisions you make can be your own. In all the confusion avoid mistakes, such as setting up unnecessary trusts or buying municipal bonds that aren't tax-exempt rather than those that are.

Use the same investment smarts you would've used before the new laws and you'll make money. For, no matter what you hear in the avalanche of information about personal finance these days, there are still several truths:

(A) You really can't take it with you.

(B) No matter how much money you accumulate, someone else will have more money or "older" money or some reason to think their money is better than yours.

(C) Someone always is willing to take your money.

Whether touting real estate bought with no money down or low-interest government loans, playing the new issues market or stashing away junk bonds, many investment salespeople are presenting formulas as fact these days. The problem is that many fancy schemes that worked took a lot of luck, occurred when conditions were different, or required almost total dedication on the part of the investor. Spending hundreds of dollars on inspirational tapes on selling techniques won't help much if the goals presented for real estate were projected when price appreciation was running at a different pace. Picking up money in your "spare time" won't be such a good deal if it means hundreds of hours of remodeling work or use of "special" tactics that just barely stay within, or overreach, the law. The most rational-sounding scheme to make quick dollars in exotic stocks or partnerships could wind up a heartbreaker, especially since changes in tax laws have changed the rules significantly.

It's not just a fool who is soon parted from his money. A great many intelligent people make decidedly foolish moves with their hard-earned dollars because they aren't paying attention.

Try to avoid the most common financial mistakes:

—*Delaying decisions about your money.* Millions of Americans pledge each year to do more to invest wisely, but never get around to it. Procrastinators typically leave money in the very lowest-yielding accounts available at banks without looking into alternatives. They wait until a trend has run its course, then say it's too late to do anything anyway.

—*Not diversifying.* The stock market may get the headlines, but a thoughtful long-term plan should consider all of the other alternatives. Never put all of your eggs in one basket.

—*Not shopping around for the best deals.* Always talk to three or more institutions offering the same investment to find out what they offer. That goes for banks, savings and loans, brokerage firms, mutual fund companies or insurance firms.

—*Losing track of your money.* Many people at all income levels quite literally forget what money and assets they have. Without carefully keeping tabs on insurance policies, property and investment accounts, it's impossible to make sensible decisions about spending money or committing to new investments. Try to reassess your position monthly, or, at the very least, once a quarter.

—*Listening to the advice of only friends and neighbors.* Some people wouldn't take the advice of others on what movie to see, but they'll plunk thousands of dollars into an investment based on declarations of a "sure thing" or "sweet deal." Do your homework and take suggestions of others only as a starting point.

—*Investing without fully understanding.* Many readers of my column contact me weeks after they've put money into an investment vehicle to ask if they did the right thing. Though the amount invested may be substantial, they frequently don't understand how it works, the yield or how soon they can get their money back. Never invest in anything you don't understand!

—*Paying too much in fees.* Banks and investment firms are trying their darndest to slap as many fees and commissions as possible on investments. Sometimes the specifics can be found only in a prospectus or brochure, and even then they are obscurely worded. Demand information about all fees and, if they are unreasonable, take your money elsewhere.

—*Not keeping other family members informed.* Family members, and spouses in particular, should know generally what's being done investment-wise. It's amazing how many surviving spouses discover investments they didn't know existed or, worse yet, investments they thought they had that aren't there anymore.

Helping to get this book rolling were the thousands of letters received from the readers of my syndicated newspaper column around the country. One of my three weekly columns deals solely with reader queries, so it's easy for me to gauge their interests.

New tax laws have been part of their concern lately. But how these laws affect their investment interests is more far-ranging than mere statutes, and so is the scope of this book. Americans also have a lively sense of humor, so hopefully I can lighten the load of financial worry with a joke or two within these pages.

For example, one fellow writing a letter to my column was straightforward enough.

Dear Mr. Leckey:
My brother-in-law drives a Cadillac Eldorado, owns a
$275,000 home and vacations for three weeks each year
in Florida. For the life of me, I can't figure how he does
it. What do you think? I compute his regular income
from his job to be as follows . . .

That letter may be an unusual example (you know, the
brother-in-law really was living too well). It is interesting to
note that many questions I receive are much the same,
whether they come from New York, Chicago or Los Angeles,
or other cities such as Denver, Hartford or Ft. Lauderdale.

Readers tend to ask basic questions about prospects for their
particular stock or handling a tax problem, or they seek specific information on an investment. Some requests come in
strange forms. I've received dozens of postcards depicting bi-
kini-clad models at the beach or swimming pool. Despite such
a buildup, each card simply had a straightforward question
about a stock penned on the reverse side. They were sent, no
doubt, from hotel rooms amid nagging worry over whether
expensive vacations could be afforded.

A lot of folks must write letters while at the office, since
they don't hesitate to use office stationery. They often cross
out the printed lettering, as in the case of one congressman
who crossed out each of his listed committee assignments with
a black magic marker. As many questions as possible that are
considered representative or interesting are answered in my
weekly question-and-answer column, or serve as a spring-
board for a regular column. Or, in this case, even a book.

No, Americans don't care only about taxes, so this book
covers the entire scope of investment.

The Beatles in their song "Taxman" two decades ago told
of the woes of giving the government its due: "If you get too
cold, I'll tax the heat; if you take a walk, I'll tax your feet.
'Cause I'm the taxman, yeah, I'm the taxman."

Giving Uncle Sam his due under the new tax laws, you can
still make money.

2   Expert Advice

The experts are ready when you are.

Wall Street pundits have plenty of advice about the new laws and how they affect the investor's ability to make money.

The many crosscurrents in this new game plan from Washington, however, can make either going for high yields or seeking tax-exempt returns the right move, depending on the individual.

"I've put together a few things worth noting as all of this tax change has unfolded," said Maynard Engel, director of personal financial management for E.F Hutton & Co., as he walked over to his desk to pick up a 4-inch-thick folder crammed full of memos on the new tax laws.

"In a nutshell,the new tax laws dramatically change the investing habits of Americans," he said. "There will be a heavy shift away from debt and toward short-term capital gains, a strong emphasis upon investment income versus growth."

The transition won't come easily, however. Say what you will about the long-term positive effects of federal tax overhaul, its short-term effects have produced more pain then gain on Wall Street. Top strategists point out that, combined with economic uncertainties, the fallout from the new laws is dramatic. "Tax reform played a role in any market declines in

1986, since the investor had good reason to sell before year end because of capital gains (more favorable in 1986 than 1987)," said Leon Cooperman, cochairman of the investment policy committee of Goldman, Sachs & Co., throwing up his hands to emphasize the irony of it all. From now on, future increases in tax rates seem far more likely than any reductions, Cooperman reasons.

"The amazing things about tax reform are that Congress actually did it and that it will produce incredible disequilibrium that we can't even begin to assess yet," said Stanley Salvigsen, former chief investment strategist for Merrill Lynch & Co., who recently opened his own money management firm. He believes that lower tax rates mean bonds and other fixed-rate investments such as bank certificates may be more attractive than stocks. Attempts to turn borrowers into savers overnight may have a negative effect on consumer-driven industries and the economy, he worries.

"Tax reform will do for yuppies what the railroad did for the buffalo," Salvigsen said with a laugh. "This country will no longer be geared to debt-based consumption and credit will be used more sparingly."

Edward Yardeni, director of economics for Prudential-Bache Securities, is convinced tax revision is a short-term negative for the economy that at least should help keep interest rates low for a while. He's cynical enough to expect tax brackets will be raised "in a year or two." Indicative of investment shifts, Yardeni and his wife in the fall of 1986 invested a sum of money in—can you believe it?—Series EE U.S savings bonds (before the government cut the guaranteed minimum rate).

New tax laws are having other distinct effects on the markets. "We're seeing and will continue to see a preference by individuals toward high-yield securities," said Steve Einhorn, cochairman of the investment policy committee at Goldman, Sachs. The overriding positive about reform, to Einhorn's way of thinking, is that it represents a shift to financial assets such as stocks and bonds, away from real assets such as real estate and tax shelters. In the long run, that's good for the markets.

Portfolio managers of big mutual funds told me that not only funds specializing in high-dividend stocks and bonds but also tax-exempt municipal bonds will be the fund stars of the late 1980s, indicative of different people benefiting from different tax brackets. The municipal bond salespeople have been signing up new investors in droves, as they point out that individual brackets won't be coming down as quickly or as far as many high-income Americans had expected.

It is the concept of tax shelters that has become the most unacceptable under today's laws, which place emphasis on making money instead of sheltering it. As a result, a new breed of investments has been spawned.

The panoramic view of New York City from James Carthaus' 102nd-floor office at Shearson Lehman Brothers in the World Trade Center is truly spectacular. Not that he enjoys it much, however. "Frankly, I never look," he explained somewhat sheepishly, his eyes averting the long windows. "I've always been afraid of heights and still am."

Carthaus, you see, has adapted to his circumstances, just as the limited partnership business he oversees for Shearson has adapted to the worrisome world of the new tax laws. Tax shelters with big losses are out; a wide variety of income-producing partnerships investing in everything from cable television to real estate are in. "Our volume of partnerships is up over last year, as we shift away from shelters for big clients to income partnerships for smaller investors," said Carthaus, director of financial services. "Another trend is shortening the length of partnerships to 5 years, down from 7 to 10 years."

Shelters fall under a phase-in rule that allows investors to use 65 percent of writeoffs in 1987 and dwindling percentages from then on. This means some syndicators of existing partnerships have been hurriedly restructuring to provide income and less debt for investors already committed long-term. Real estate partnerships are being constructed with cash, since tax revision lengthens the depreciable life of real estate and reduces tax benefits available in any one year. In addition, publicly-traded real estate investment trusts (REITs), which manage a portfolio of real estate to earn profits for shareholders, are expected to gain in popularity. So will publicly-traded master limited partnerships that combine real estate investments designed for tax shelter with those that provide income to benefit the investor.

The new tax laws may result in some other structural changes in investing.

Some American stock investors, for example, may be tempted to become wheeler-dealers now that the new tax laws have removed the distinction between short-term and long-term capital gains. Though the tax penalty for more active trading is removed, being a short-term thinker still won't lead down the path to riches. Best results still belong to investors who hold on to their stocks for the long haul, rather than the active traders.

Few people do well trading on a short-term basis. Changing the capital gains treatment won't alter that reality. Al Frank, editor of the Prudent Speculator, P.O. Box 1767, Santa Monica, Calif. 90406, has posted an amazing 682 percent gain in the portfolio he's recommended during the 1980s. No other newsletter comes close to that, according to the Washington, D.C.-based Hulbert Financial Digest which tracks a $10,000 hypothetical portfolio for each investment letter.

"I think the stock market will be different under tax reform, with trades occurring more frequently, and I really wonder if that's good," said Frank, who selects undervalued stocks and then bides his time. "Trying to catch market turns is wrong."

For example, Frank has held Zayre Corp. stock in his portfolio nearly nine years, during which it split a number of times and increased in value by 2,900 percent. Of the 334 stocks Frank has recommended in nine years, 268 have shown gains, 65 have had losses and one is unchanged. That's an 80 percent winning percentage for being patient.

Charles Allmon, editor of Growth Stock Outlook, P.O. Box 15381, Chevy Chase, Md. 20815, his portfolio up 256 percent since 1980, is urging his subscribers to be patient enough to invest in oil company stocks "because seven years down the road, you might see a payoff of two to 10 times on your money." In the meantime, he's counseling them to unload their tax shelters because of the new tax laws.

"Stocks and bonds in general will be more attractive under tax reform, just as real estate and tax shelters will be less attractive," predicted Marty Zweig, editor of Zweig Forecast, 900 Third Ave., New York, N.Y.10022. His portfolio is up 253 percent since 1980 by employing a lot of short-term trading to produce long-term results. "While I think there will be one bear market before 1990, I'm convinced the stock market will hit the 3,000 level in five years." Zweig feels there are too many risk-oriented investors these days. Yet he's quick to point out that his portfolio is aggressive enough to be heavily in stocks right now, so he's "hardly sitting in T-bills."

Value Line OTC Special Situations newsletter, 711 Third Ave., New York, N.Y. 10017, its portfolio up 210 percent the last six years on success of small-company stocks, has seen Community Psychiatric Centers stock rise 4,000 percent since it was first recommended in 1977. Editor Peter Shraga says his newsletter sticks with picks "through thick and thin." He's so long-suffering as to believe that technology stocks, depressed in the last three years, will be on the comeback trail in the late 1980s.

Meanwhile, James Dines, editor of Dines Letter, P.O. Box 22, Belvedere, Calif. 94920, remains proud of the fact that he recommended gold at $35 an ounce in the 1960s. The average of his portfolio is up 208 percent since 1980 primarily because he spotted the trend to deflation and moved out of tired industries such as agriculture and steel.

Dines' advice for dealing with the new tax laws is clear. "Make a lot of capital gains and don't worry about taxes," he declared. "The strongest strategy for the rest of this decade will be to invest in food stocks and other deflation hedges, such as banks and insurance companies. I'm convinced that real estate and petroleum are dead."

Everyone must cope with the changes, but some companies and stocks will do better than others.

Shortly after President Reagan signed the tax changes into law, Sen. Bob Packwood was given a box of Wheaties from an executive of General Mills, maker of the "breakfast of champions." It had a picture of Packwood himself on the front because he was a "true champion" for pushing tax reform, the executive explained. It's not hard to figure out such enthusiasm for the revisions. Food companies you see, happen to be in one of the industries that prospers the most under the changes in the tax laws.

Picking the right companies and investments is tough, however. Many American investors, who have alternately felt the thrill of victory and the agony of defeat during the 1980's, are now biting their nails over the new tax laws and an uncertain economic environment for the companies in which they invest.

So how does one approach investing for the remainder of the 1980s?

Carefully. Very carefully. Especially in the stock market, where some companies will reap rich rewards from changing times while others come up dry.

From several prognosticators of proven mettle, I requested five stock selections apiece that they expect to do well the remainder of this decade. No stock can ever be a sure thing, but emphasis was placed on those with the fewest negatives.

"Tax reform, sluggish economic growth and a generally weak U.S. dollar will provide a boost for some time to firms in cosmetics, drugs, leisure, newspapers, restaurants, food and retailing," said Elaine Garzarelli, director of sector analysis for Shearson. "Look for those with superior growth that are cheap."

Her "five for the '80s" are:

— Alberto-Culver (traded on the New York Stock Exchange), in hair-care and beauty aids

— Forest Labs (American Stock Exchange), manufacturer of pharmaceuticals

— Walt Disney Productions (NYSE), famous for amusement parks, films and television ventures

— Brunswick Corp. (NYSE), in marine and recreation products

— Sizzler Restaurants International (sold over the counter), the steak-house restaurant franchiser.

"Lots of companies won't be doing well in what will be a deteriorating atmosphere of American financial markets, so the investor must be in first-class growth companies," advised William Gillard, portfolio strategist for Kidder, Peabody & Co., who considers tax reform a negative, particularly for 1987. "Pharmaceutical companies, for example, are the best major industry in the United States, and they aren't threatened by any Japanese competition."

Solid bets for the remainder of the 1980s, Gillard predicts, are:

— Merck & Co. (NYSE), in drugs and chemicals

— Bristol-Myers (NYSE), in toiletries and drugs

— Dun & Bradstreet (NYSE), in business information, publishing and television

— Waste Management (NYSE), in solid and chemical waste services

— Masco Corp. (NYSE), in building and home improvement products.

"Tax reform in the long run will be bullish for stocks, and some companies that suffered from high taxes will prosper after the changes," said Zweig of the Zweig Forecast. "Drug stocks, publishing, service and financial companies should be looking good."

He expects good performances from:

— Dreyfus Corp. (NYSE), of mutual fund fame

— Contel Corp. (NYSE), a telecommunications company operating in 30 states

— NYNEX Corp. (NYSE), the regional telephone company in New York and New England

— AMR Corp. (NYSE), holding company for American Airlines

— Georgia-Pacific (NYSE), in plywood, lumber and paper.

"I see a 3,500 Dow sometime in the 1980s, and I expect companies that didn't have the investment tax credit (which was abolished under reform) to do particuarly well," said Frank, editor of the Prudent Speculator. "I especially think low and stable interest rates will be a boon to savings and loans."

Stocks that Frank feels will be successful the next several years include:

— Chrysler Corp. (NYSE)

— CalFed Inc. (NYSE), holding company for banking and insurance

— Lockheed Corp. (NYSE), aircraft, missiles and space

— Nortek Inc. (NYSE), manufacturer of textiles and conduit

— Radice Corp. (NYSE), home and apartment building developer operating in the southeastern part of the country.

Those are expert opinions, to be sure. But the average investor can take heart from Frank's advice on becoming successful at long-term investing.

"I wasn't a broker, a business major or a banker, so I didn't think I was qualified," Frank relates. "Yet I found out that real investment success simply consists of learning about the market and following a discipline."

When I was a graduate fellow at Columbia University a few years back, economist John Kenneth Galbraith was a guest at one of our regular dinner sessions. One enterprising classmate asked the august economist what courses we should take in the business school the following term.

Galbraith raised an eyebrow and then replied: "My goodness, don't you people have counselors for that sort of thing?"

In other words, don't bother the experts until you've spent some time doing your homework. And, now that you've gotten the word from the top on how to make money, it is time to become your own expert.

3   The New Tax Laws

A cartoon parody of a famous junk mail campaign depicts a six-foot-tall frankfurter, humanized with arms and legs, as it opens a mailbox. The envelope pulled from the box reads: "YOU may already be a WEINER!"

The familiar promotion that the cartoon spoofs is the one claiming to give every American a chance to be a mega-buck "WINNER" of a sweepstakes. It's another in a long line of modern American events in which one is either a winner or a loser, with nothing much in between.

One professional football team will win the Super Bowl each year and be a winner; every other team is deemed by society to be a loser.

The new tax laws have become part of that syndrome. Recently I was walking down the street, in a hurry to get to an interview, when a woman, 50-ish, flagged me down. "Andrew, I watched your report on the new tax laws on television last night and it was very nice," she said as she extended her hand. "But, what I really want to know is: Who wins?"

She's not alone in her curiosity. As we all watched the authors of reform toast their efforts with champagne after the final vote, we weren't really sure whether we should be happy as they were. A happy politician, we have all learned, does not necessarily mean joyous things are happening.

We asked ourselves: Will this make it tougher for me to make money?

Figuring out who wins is no easy task. It's true that most Americans will pay federal taxes at lower rates at the end of the phase-in period in 1988. But, as we will see, lower rates do not necessarily mean paying less tax. As a commercial for one investment firm points out: "It's not what you make, it's what you keep that counts."

It's also true that millions of the poor will be taken from the tax rolls because of larger personal exemptions and standard deductions. That's a definite plus. But for many middle-income folks, the trim in their tax won't counteract the tax breaks they'll lose on state and local sales tax, consumer interest, capital gains and IRAs. Ironically, those lucky enough to make astonishing sums such as $1 million a year will actually reap substantial tax savings from rate reductions under the new tax laws.

The problem is that all the "good stuff" of the new tax laws is phased in, while the "bad stuff" in which deductions were lost happened right off the bat in 1987. Another is that many savvy folks have actively used shelters to cut their tax burden in the past and will miss those tools. An estimated 40 percent of all tax returns with income between $50,000 and $75,000 will face an increase. Fifty-five percent of those reporting income of $75,000 to $100,000 will also be facing federal tax hikes.

To make matters worse, you'd better be prepared for some intricate "transition" IRS forms that'll have your head spinning when you begin to figure out whether you've won or lost.

On the basic scoreboard, we might say that parents saving for their children's college education lose big because income-shifting techniques are curtailed. Many believe this will trigger a move to tax-exempt and growth investments for children, rather than high-income instruments that are now popular.

Homeowners are winners, since they retain their deductions—although for many they'll be received at less advantageous lower tax rates. Families in which both spouses work are losers, in that they will no longer have the ability to exclude up to $3,000 of what they earn. A car loan becomes a decreasingly sensible proposition as the amount deductible is gradually phased out. What Americans owe in state taxes could be heading upward too, because many states collect taxes based on federal returns. Elimination of many tax breaks means state tax rates will be applied to bigger amounts of taxable income. In many cases, it looks like the states could be big winners.

As you can see, it is a mixed bag. These are tax laws subject to few broad generalizations and requiring a definite need to do one's individual homework.

"You know what's ironic?" one tax accountant asked rhetorically. "The new tax laws couldn't have come into being without the modern computer. And, more than ever, the average Joe is going to need someone to do a computer run before he even knows where he stands."

Music to the ears of an accountant, perhaps, but no deal for the average Joe or Josephine. I hope this book gives you a running start at successfully handling the new laws on your own.

In a nutshell

The main idea of the government as far as individuals are concerned is to consolidate the rate schedule and lower tax rates. So, instead of 14 rates ranging from 11 to 50 percent for married couples as in the past, in 1988 there will be only two rates of 15 and 28 percent. But it's not so simple or sweet a deal as it seems. Most families with taxable income over $71,900, or $43,150 for single individuals, will be subject to an additional 5 percent surcharge, making their true marginal rate 33 percent. In 1987, there's a five-bracket rate structure with rates ranging from 11 to 38.5 percent.

With surcharges and special 1987 rates, many people making tax plans based on a 28 percent tax bracket are in for a sad surprise.

The personal exemption rises to $1,900 in 1987, $1,950 in 1988 and $2,000 in 1989. The zero bracket amount is converted to a standard deduction. It is increased in 1988 to $5,000 for a married couple and $3,000 for a single individual. All of this obviously isn't simply a gift from above. To pay for the reduction in tax rates and increases in the personal exemption and the standard deduction, the law increases corporate taxes. While this sounds like a boon for the individual, just about everyone realizes these days that what affects corporations ultimately affects their workers and the cost of the goods sold to the consumer.

Some old favorites of taxpayers have been sent packing. The two-earner deduction, income averaging, the dividends-received deduction and the political contributions credit are repealed. In a major defeat for many high-powered lobbying groups, the deductible individual retirement account contributions are restricted. The floor under the medical deduction is increased. Most miscellaneous itemized deductions, plus certain unreimbursed employee business expenses, are subject to a new 2 percent (of adjusted gross income) floor.

Your home is still handy, but sales taxes will no longer be the taxpayer's friend. Mortgage interest on the taxpayer's principal residence and second residence remains deductible on loans up to the purchase price plus the cost of improvements, with a further exception for loans to finance educational and medical expenses. The sales tax deduction is repealed. Itemized deductions remain for other state and local income and property taxes. Appreciation on charitable gifts of property may trigger the alternative minimum tax.

The entire strategy surrounding capital gains is thrown up for grabs. Capital gains will be taxed in full, except that in 1987 the maximum tax rate in capital gains will be limited to 28 percent. The deduction for investment interest is limited to investment income. Also, passive losses from real estate and tax shelters other than oil and gas working interests are allowed to offset only income from similar passive investments. That means that tax shelters can no longer fully offset salary, dividend and interest income. The alternative minimum tax for individuals is strengthened and the rate is increased to 21 percent.

Though the overall reduction in individual income taxes will average five percent, taxpayers at the lower end of the income scale will have above-average tax decreases, primarily due to the increases in the personal exemption and the standard deduction. About one-fifth of all tax payers, however, will have a tax increase. Two-earner families who have no dependents and lose the IRA deduction and high-earners who make heavy use of tax shelters or often realize large capital gains will have tax increases. For 1987, many more high-income taxpayers will have a tax increase because the tax rate reductions on ordinary income are phased in over two years but the repeal of many tax incentives takes effect immediately.

You win some, you lose some.

Stay in shape

No matter how much you know about the new taxes, talk about the new taxes or worry about the new taxes, putting your financial records in order is still the most important way to gain control of your taxes. Don't use tax reform as an excuse to flip out, or to give total responsibility to the person who counsels you or prepares your taxes. Besides sparing yourself hours of time and plenty of frustration, a little organization also will ensure that you get all the tax breaks you deserve. Reform has made that a more arduous task, all the more reason to stay in shape financially.

Many taxpayers buy elaborate log books and files or expensive computer programs, arming themselves to the teeth. That's fine, as long as you keep everything up to date. But you can do just as well with a less elaborate system that is neither hooked to a computer nor part of a three-volume set featuring color-coded worksheets.

The tried and true "envelope" system, for example, does fine. It consists of envelopes marked for major categories. You put in receipts and canceled checks that have some tax significance. Make sure that you keep only what is necessary, rather than just tossing in every receipt. By putting receipts and documents in marked categories, you'll wind up with only the meaningful information needed to substantiate your tax claims. Keep everything at least as long as the three years from the date of filing that your return is subject to Internal Revenue Service scrutiny.

People often put their records back into a big box after they've prepared their taxes and forget about them. If you've done something complicated in a given year, you should put a note with your records explaining what the situation was. Because, if you're audited two years later, you might not remember all those particulars. Consider your own tax personality. Many Americans keep virtually no tax records and then try desperately to reconstruct everything at tax time. Many others squirrel away everything and have to wade through stacks of paper, much of which has little or no relevance.

It's a good idea to do a tax analysis of your situation quarterly, looking at your income and projecting it through the rest of the year. Remember that even the major changes of tax reform don't change the basics of keeping track of your financial situation. Right now is the right time to do some comparisons of your tax liability before tax changes go into effect, during transition and after they are completed. This book will later provide some examples and advice to help out with that task.

Surviving a tax audit

The IRS has its share of problems these days. It has survived the computer foul-ups of several years ago, but now finds the new tax laws are requiring it to revise most of its 511 forms, update its 102 publications, rewrite thousands of computer programs and redo its regulations. But it had been doing mock-ups of all of this during the reform procedure in Congress and even advised reformers on what could and couldn't be done effectively.

So no, the IRS is not so burdened with all the tax changes that it will forget one of its major roles: auditing taxpayer returns. And no, the fact that so much is new and that there are so many transitional rules doesn't mean you'll have a ready excuse if you've goofed. Also, remember that the new tax puts more teeth in tax penalties, which means your mistakes can come back to haunt you. Those penalty rules apply to all returns filed starting in 1987.

"Why me?" That's the usual anguished reaction when a taxpayer receives a tax audit notice in the mail from the IRS. The worry of just such an audit subconsciously eats away at millions of taxpayers—no matter how honest they may be—as they put together their income tax forms this time of year. After all, one frets that some major error will be made that could trigger a lengthy audit and wind up costing thousands of dollars or sending the poor taxpayer "up the river" in disgrace.

How do you survive a tax audit? "I'd counsel anyone who receives an audit notice in the mail to relax," said one IRS auditor with a decade of experience. "Just be sure to put together the documentation that's requested and be able to back up your deductions."

Less than 2 percent of individual returns are ever audited. In reviewing returns by computer, the IRS gives values to different items reported on your return and a greater score can increase the likelihood of your being audited. In addition, there is also a random-selection system that selects other returns so the IRS can gauge overall taxpayer compliance. Consider a tax audit to be just like the Army and provide information only about what you are asked, advises one tax accountant. Don't volunteer information in any other areas.

In many cases, additional information is simply requested and the entire matter can be cleared up in the mail. Other times, you'll be scheduled to an hour-long audit appointment at a local IRS office. Whether you bring your tax preparer with you or go by yourself depends on the complexity of the problem. However, some individuals are better off not going to an audit because they may wind up nervously going off on a tangent that unnecessarily raises other questions, or they'll wind up in an argument that is truly counterproductive. If your case requires a great deal of documentation or also involves a business which you own, the audit may be conducted in your home or office.

"When I got the notice I gulped out loud, but it turned out to be a line-by-line audit that had simply been chosen by computer with no real complaint," said one taxpayer who was audited recently. "However, I did wind up having to write up a log of some things I hadn't done when I should have."

The chance of avoiding scrutiny is increased if you double-check all mathematical computations before you send in your form, making certain all items are listed on the proper line. Do that as you prepare your return, so that you won't have to worry in the event you are audited. If you haven't kept the necessary documentation, you probably can obtain it from whatever charity, hospital or bank is involved. Some factors that tend to boost the likelihood of an audit are: a high income level; unusually large deductions; large capital gains or losses on your investments; and owning your own business.

And remember: Misunderstanding the new tax laws won't be accepted as an excuse.

By-the-numbers basics

Specific tax information is not the stuff of novels, so I'll make a deal with you. If you'd rather get on to other tips in this book about handling your money and making money rather than go through the tax law basics in the rest of this chapter, go ahead. Just realize that these nuts and bolts are important and well worth going over later, or using as a reference as you plot your strategy under the new tax laws. The biggest mistake taxpayers make is not setting their tax strategies soon enough, or making plans based on incorrect information. So it is worth boning up on the basics during these days of change.

The numbers game is important in figuring your taxes the next several years. For joint tax returns in 1987, taxable income up to $3,000 is in a marginal tax rate of 11 percent; $3,000 to $28,000 is taxed at 15 percent; $28,000 to $45,000 is at 28 percent; $45,000 to $90,000 is at 35 percent; and $90,000 and more is at 38.5 percent. For joint returns in 1988, up to $29,750 in taxable income is in a 15 percent marginal tax rate; and amounts above that are at 28 percent.

For single returns in 1987, taxable income up to $1,800 is in the 11 percent marginal tax rate; $1,800 to $16,800 is at 15 percent; $16,800 to $27,000 is at 28 percent; $27,000 to $54,000 is at 35 percent; and $54,000 and over is at the 38.5 percent marginal tax rate. For single returns in 1988, taxable income up to $17,850 is in the 15 percent marginal tax rate, while $17,850 and over are at 28 percent.

For 1988 and later years, there's a 5 percent surcharge on taxable income between $71,900 and $149,250 for joint returns and between $43,150 and $89,560 for single individuals. The surcharge produces the effective marginal tax rate of 33 percent. For joint returns, the 15 percent bracket on the first $29,750 of taxable income saves $3,867.50 in taxes, compared with imposing a 28 percent rate on that income. A five percent surcharge on the $77,350 of taxable income between $71,900 and $149,250 will just recapture the $3,867.50. Thus a taxpayer with $149,250 of taxable income will pay $41,790 in tax, 28 percent of $149,250.

The drop in marginal rates between 1987 and 1988 will increase the advantage of deferring income and accelerating deductible expenses. But get out the calculator, because you'll want to be careful that plans for income deferral don't push you into the alternative minimum tax. You are only subject to the alternative minimum tax if it results in a higher tax liability than the regular tax computation. Under the new law, the rate is increased from 20 to 21 percent and a number of tax preference items are added. In other words, try to avoid paying taxes, but don't try so hard as to be socked by the alternative minimum tax.

Standard deduction

The zero bracket, the initial tax bracket in which no tax was paid, is replaced by a standard deduction. For 1987, joint returns receive a standard deduction of $3,760; heads of households $2,540; single individuals $2,540; and married individuals filing separately $1,880. In 1988, joint returns receive a standard deduction of $5,000; heads of households $4,400; single individuals $3,000; and married individuals filing separately $2,500.

Personal exemption

Good for some, not so idyllic for others. The personal exemption for individuals, spouses and dependents rises to $1,900 for 1987, $1,950 for 1988; and $2,000 for 1989. The $2,000 personal exemption will be indexed for inflation beginning in 1990. The personal exemption is phased out for higher income taxpayers by imposing a 5 percent surcharge on income above certain levels. The phaseout begins at taxable income of $149,250 for joint returns, $123,790 for heads of household, $89,560 for single individuals, and $113,300 for married individuals filing separately. The phaseout range is $10,920 per exemption in 1988 and $11,200 per exemption in 1989. For a four-person family, the phaseout in 1988 ends at $192,930 of taxable income.

During the phaseout of personal exemptions, the effective marginal tax rate is 33 percent on additional dollars of income.

After personal exemptions are phased out, the marginal tax rate falls to 28 percent.

Any person eligible to be claimed as a dependent on another taxpayer's return is not permitted a personal exemption. However, to reduce the number of dependents required to file tax returns and pay tax on small amounts of income, dependents may use up to $500 of their standard deduction to offset unearned income.

The two-earner deduction is repealed, but not without some counterbalance. The flatter rate schedule and wider tax brackets reduce the marriage penalty for most two-earner couples. Because of the phaseouts of the 15 percent tax bracket and personal exemptions, however, some higher-income two-earner families will have a marriage penalty greater than under prior law.

Income averaging

Income averaging, which was designed to ease the effect of having a disproportionately high tax in a year of unusually high earnings, is done away with. Tax was figured on the average of the total income of the current year and three preceding years. Particularly for folks "on the way up" in their careers and making substantial jumps in income, this is bad news.

Individual capital gains

Changing the fundamentals. The capital gains exclusion for individuals, which produced a maximum tax rate of 20 percent on gains, is repealed. Capital gains will be taxed at the same rates as other income, but in 1987 the top capital gains rate will be limited to 28 percent by means of an alternative tax computation.

As with ordinary income, the top marginal rate on capital

gains can be as high as 33 percent if the taxpayer is in the 5 percent surcharge range.

The new laws don't actually repeal the statutory definition of capital assets, but apply the same rates to capital gains as apply to ordinary income. The previous $3,000 limitation on the deduction of net capital losses against ordinary income is retained, but, under the new law, a dollar of capital loss will offset a full dollar of ordinary income, up to the $3,000 limit without the two-for-one rules of the old law. The new law applies to gains realized before 1987 but reported on the installment method after that date. So, if you sold a capital asset in 1985 with payments due in 1987, you'll pay tax on the capital gain break you expected—not a nice surprise.

Limitations on IRA contributions

So much for the taxpayer's trust that what the government says it will do it will continue doing for the long haul. Starting in the 1987 tax year, an individual is permitted to make a tax-deductible individual retirement account contribution of $2,000 only if he or she is not a participant in a qualified pension or profit-sharing plan. Even if covered under a qualified plan, a deductible IRA contribution can be made if adjusted gross income is less than $40,000 for married couples filing jointly and $25,000 for single returns.

The $2,000 amount is phased out between $40,000 and $50,000 of adjusted gross income ($25,000 and $35,000 for singles) before taking the IRA contribution into account. Even if you do not qualify to deduct your IRA contribution, you can make a non-deductible contribution of up to $2,000 each year with no penalty. So the income earned on the IRA funds will still be tax-deferred.

401(k) Plans cut back

The maximum annual deferral an employee may elect under a 401(k) plan is sliced from $30,000 to $7,000. This is one big benefit that is significantly curtailed.

Incentive stock options

While it won't affect most Americans, there are frowns in the corporate boardrooms. Repeal of the capital gains exclusion will reduce the relative attractiveness of incentive stock options as compensation, since gain recognized on sale of stock acquired under those options will be taxed at ordinary rates. The law limits the granting of incentive stock options to grants of no more than $100,000 first exercisable in any given year. Restrictions on the order in which they may be exercised are repealed. Given repeal of capital gains, there's no incentive to hold stock after the exercise of the stock option. Executives will likely delay exercise of their stock option until close to expiration or the time they wish to sell.

Exclusions from income

It doesn't pay to be out of work or even to win the Nobel prize anymore. Unemployment compensation is fully taxed and the $100/$200 dividend exclusion is repealed. Meanwhile, awards for artistic, scientific and charitable achievement are taxed unless assigned to a charity. Employee productivity awards are treated as compensation and the exclusion for scholarships is limited to the amount of tuition and course-required fees, books and supplies awarded to degree candidates. The employee education assistance exclusion is extended through 1987 and the limit is increased to $5,250. The dependent care assistance exclusion is limited to $5,000 or $2,500 for married couples filing separately. The prepaid legal services exclusion is extended through 1987.

Itemized and other deductions

Medical expenses and health insurance. The floor under the medical expense deduction is increased from 5 to 7.5 percent of the taxpayer's adjusted gross income. Self-employed individuals can deduct 25 percent of the amounts paid for health insurance on behalf of themselves (but not more than self-employment income) and on dependents, if those individuals are not eligible to participate in an employer-subsidized health plan. The provision is effective for taxable years beginning in 1987, 1988 and 1989.

State and local taxes. The itemized deduction for state and local sales taxes is repealed. However, sales taxes and other nonfederal taxes which are not allowed as an itemized deduction and which are attributable to the purchase of business property are added to the basis of the property for depreciation purposes. The deduction for state and local income and property taxes is unchanged.

Interest expense. The act disallows any deduction for personal interest, such as interest on credit card debt for personal expenses, car loans and tax deficiencies. Mortgage interest on the taxpayer's principal and one other residence is deductible to the extent the mortgage does not exceed the cost of the home plus improvements unless the debt was incurred prior to Aug. 17, 1986. Interest on additional mortgage indebtedness (up to fair market value) incurred for qualified educational or medical expenses can also be deducted. In addition, investment interest may be deducted only to the extent of investment income. Investment interest is interest on debts incurred to acquire or carry investments. Investment income includes dividends and interest.

The disallowance of personal interest is phased in over five year. In 1987, 35 percent of previously deductible interest is non-deductible. The disallowance increases to 60 percent in 1988, 80 percent in 1989, 90 percent in 1990 and 100 percent in later years.

Charitable deduction. For taxpayers who itemize, the deduction for charitable contributions is unchanged except that the cost of certain charitable travel is no longer deductible. Also, untaxed appreciation on charitable gifts such as stocks is included in the base of the alternative minimum tax. The charitable deduction for non-itemizers is ended. Many charities are concerned that the steep decline in tax rates and the corresponding increase in the tax cost of philanthropy will reduce charitable giving.

Casualty and theft losses. Taxpayers must by law now file timely insurance claims in order to claim a casualty deduction. If a taxpayer fails to pursue a claim for fear of a rate increase, no deduction is permitted.

Employee business expenses and miscellaneous deductions. Employee business expenses, other than those reimbursed, are permitted only as itemized deductions. Furthermore, the itemized deductions for unreimbursed, business expenses and miscellaneous deductions are allowed only to the extent they exceed 2 percent of adjusted gross income.

Some employee business expenses and miscellaneous deductions are deductible as itemized deductions but not subject to the 2 percent floor. These are moving expenses; work expenses incurred by handicapped workers; estate taxes incurred as a result of a decedent's income; amortizable bond premiums; interest expenses of short sales; expenses incurred by cooperative housing corporations; amounts included in the prior year's gross income because the taxpayer was deemed to have unrestricted rights; certain terminated annuity payments; and gambling losses to the extent of gambling winnings.

Expenses for travel and entertainment. Deductions for business meal and entertainment expenses are limited to 80 percent of the amount incurred. Those expenses not subject to the 80 percent limit on deductibility include items taxed as compensation to the recipient; expenditures for which the taxpayer receives reimbursement (the 80 percent limit is applied to the party reimbursing the taxpayer); recreational expenses such as a company picnic paid on behalf of the employees; items made available to the general public; or certain meals in a banquet setting in 1987 and 1988.

Meals. Expansion of requirements for deductiblity of business meals to conform with current rules for the deductibility of entertainment expenses. Business meals are deductible only if business is discussed before, during or after the meal, and the meal has a clear business purpose directly related to the active conduct of the taxpayer's trade or business.

Entertainment. It's just no fun anymore. There are special restrictions on entertainment expenses. The deduction for ticket cost is limited to 80 percent of face value, while a premium added to the cost of sports tickets for charitable fundraising events is deductible.

Deductions for the rental or use of a luxury skybox at a sports arena, if used by the taxpayer for more than one event, are also limited to 80 percent of the cost of regular tickets. Disallowance of the skybox deduction is phased in during taxable years beginning in 1987 and 1988 with one-third disallowed in 1987 and two-thirds disallowed in 1988. In addition, deductions for luxury water transportation are limited to twice the highest federal per diem for U.S. travel, multiplied by the number of days in transit.

Travel. Deductions are eliminated for expenses incurred for travel as a form of education; charitable travel that is for personal, recreational or vacation purposes; or the expenses of attending a convention or seminar for investment purposes.

Two percent floor. Otherwise allowable travel, meals and entertainment expenses will be grouped with miscellaneous deductions and be subject to the 2 percent of adjusted-gross-income floor. As a result, the taxpayer may not be able to fully use the 80 percent deduction for meals and entertainment expenses.

That's not all, folks: The new law also repeals the deduction for certain adoption expenses; repeals the credit for political contributions; permits ministers and military personnel a full deduction for mortgage interest and real property taxes; and tightens the hobby loss and home office deduction rules.

Income shifting, trusts and estates

And your child thought you were putting all of that money in his bank account just because you liked him, eh? Times are changing. The new law significantly restricts a parent's ability to lower the effective tax rate on investment income by transferring assets to a child. As we've explained earlier, investment income over $1,000 for children under age 14 is taxed to the child as if it were the parent's bracket. The tax is calculated by determining what the parent's tax would have been if the child's net unearned income were added to the parent's taxable income. The provision will apply not only to transfers made in the future, but also to income generated from past transfers, including those to irrevocable trusts.

In addition to essentially raising taxes for many families, this new rule adds complexity and perhaps even family jealousy. Parents will first have to do an "as if" calculation of their return before doing the child's return. Mom and dad must figure the difference between their tax if junior's income is included, and the actual tax without that income. Only then can the child's return be completed. In addition, if there is more than one child under 14 with unearned income, a pro-ration calculation to determine their tax must be made. As for family jealousy, think of Bob, age 12, and his sister Judy, age 15. On equal amounts of unearned income, Bob will pay more in tax than his sister only because he is under age 14. One more reason for him to hate his sister!

The first $500 of a child's unearned income and any amount of income earned by the child are not subject to these rules. Also, the child's unearned income can be offset by any itemized deductions attributable to it or by up to $500 of the child's standard deduction. Thus only a child's unearned income in excess of $1,000 will be subject to the new rules. Beginning in 1988, these $500 amounts will be adjusted for inflation. A child whose parent qualifies to claim him as a dependent is not entitled to claim a personal exemption on his tax return.

Trusts. The rate structure for non-grantor trusts is revised to reduce the benefits from income-splitting. The first $5,000 of taxable income of the trust is taxed at 15 percent, with any excess taxed at 28 percent. In addition, the benefit of the 15 percent rate is phased out between $13,000 and $26,000 of such income.

Prior law provided a rather complex set of rules requiring the person who created a trust to pay tax on the income of that trust. The rules now classify as grantor trusts two special trusts that had previously escaped these provisions, the Clifford trust and the spousal remainder trust. These will no longer be useful income-shifting devices.

All trusts, other than tax-exempt trusts and wholly charitable trusts, must adopt a calendar year as their taxable year. Trusts are now required to pay estimated taxes in the same way that individuals do.

Estates. The undistributed income of estates is taxed at the same rates as trusts. The law now also requires estates to make estimated income tax payments. Estates are not required to pay estimated taxes for their first two taxable years, however. Any amount not paid as estimated taxes may no longer be paid in four quarterly installments, but must be paid in full on the due date of the estate's income tax return.

These rate changes are effective July 1, 1987. The 1987 returns will use a schedule that blends the old and new rates. Changes in grantor trust rules are generally effective for transfers in trusts made after March 1, 1986. The change in taxable year rules is effective beginning after Dec. 31, 1986. Net income distributed to beneficiaries in a short taxable year is included in the beneficiary's income over a four-year period. The requirement that trusts and estates pay estimated taxes became effective for 1987.

Estimated tax payments

The individual estimated tax payment requirement is increased from 80 percent to 90 percent of the portion of the current year's tax liability. The alternative test of 100 percent of the preceding year's liability remains unchanged.

Depreciation and investment credit

Business property placed in service after Dec. 31, 1985 is no longer eligible for the investment tax credit, a dollar-for-dollar reduction of tax for up to 10 percent of the cost of certain business equipment. The rules for depreciation of business property and real estate owned for business or investment purposes have changed. These rules generally apply for property placed in service after Dec. 31, 1986. The mechanics of computing depreciation on business cars, furniture, fixtures and equipment have changed, but the result will be about the same. The big change is computing depreciation on real estate. No longer will real estate be written off over 19 years, which under old law produced large depreciation deductions. Now residential rental property must be written off over 27½ years and commercial property over 31½ years. These changes take away some of the tax incentive for owning rental real estate.

Limitations on passive losses and credits

Big changes in strategy here and a new set of definitions as well. An investor may not offset net losses from "passive activities" against income from sources other than passive activities. Credits from passive activities may not be used to offset tax arising from other than passive activities. Passive activities are defined as those in which the taxpayer doesn't materially participate, as well as rental activities. An individual participates in an activity if he or she is actively involved in its day-to-day operations. Limited partnerships are deemed passive activities and portfolio income such as dividends and interest is not income from a passive activity. A working interest (direct ownership) in oil and gas activities is not subject to these limitations.

With few exceptions, the overall limitations on passive losses and credits apply in full for tax years starting with 1987 for passive activities entered after Oct. 22, 1986. For passive activities entered before the date of enactment, passive loss rules are phased in over a five-year period, by disallowing progressively larger percentages of passive activity credits and net losses incurred during those years. These are 35 percent in 1987, 60 percent in 1980, 80 percent in 1989, 90 percent in 1990 and 100 percent in 1991.

Losses and credits disallowed are considered suspended, and carried forward until there is income or tax from passive activities against which they can be used. Suspended losses can be used against any income in the year in which an investor makes a qualifying disposition of his entire interest in the passive activity which created them. Suspended credits may generally be used only against tax liability attributable to income from passive activities.

There's an exception to the passive loss limitations for individuals who actively participate in real estate rental activities. The law says that a taxpayer owning 10 percent or less of a rental activity is not considered an active participant in it, and that an interest of a limited partner will not be considered an interest in which the partner actively participates. Active real estate investors may deduct up to $25,000 of losses or equivalent credits against income from non-passive sources. This exception is phased out by 50 percent of the amount by which adjusted gross income exceeds $100,000. The phaseout results in no deductions for losses from real estate rental activities for individuals with adjusted gross incomes of more than $150,000.

In addition, individuals who invest in low-income housing and historic rehabilitations are an exception. Tax on non-passive income of up to $25,000 may be offset by credits from these projects, even if the taxpayer wasn't personally active in the business that generated the credits. This is phased out at the rate of 50 percent of the amount by which adjusted gross income exceeds $200,000. When adjusted gross income exceeds $250,000, no low-income or historic rehabilitation credits are allowed.

Investment interest deductions

The law limits deductibility of any interest expense other than that incurred in a trade or business. It does away with the

$10,000 in interest deductions allowed in excess of investment income, and expands the interest subject to the limitation. It modifies the definition of investment income against which investment interest expense may be deducted. Interest and income from activities subject to the passive loss limitations is not treated as investment interest or income. During the phase-in of the passive loss limitations, however, any passive losses taken against non-passive income reduce the amount of income considered as investment income. The new investment interest limitations are phased in over the next five years in the same manner as the consumer interest and passive loss limitations.

Tax shelter registration

Effective in 1987, a tax shelter is considered an investment with a greater than two-to-one ratio of the deductions plus 350 percent of the credits to the amount invested. It increases the penalty for failure to register a tax shelter to 1 percent of the amount invested. It also increases the penalty for failure to report a tax shelter identification number on a tax return from $50 to $250. There's an increase in the penalty on underpayments of tax attributable to tax shelters from 10 to 20 percent, effective for returns due after Dec. 31, 1986.

You made it!

Honda may make it simple, but Congress seldom does. As you can see if you've perused the tax changes this far, the new laws may be an advance in making taxation more equitable but it is definitely not simplification.

Under the new tax laws, for example, the proverbial three martini lunch may become a 2.4 martini lunch. That's because new rules on travel and entertainment expenses allow you to deduct only 80 percent of the cost of business meals. While your company may reimburse you for the entire meal, expect the cut in employer's deductions to make your boss much more of a tightwad when it comes to your expense account. Carry-out pizza, anyone?

The new W-4 employee withholding form and instructions used to calculate taxes to be withheld from pay has grown from two pages to four pages. While many workers, single or married to a nonworking spouse, can stop at line "E," the worksheet requires others to go all the way to line "U." Be sure to file it as soon as possible and withhold from future paychecks at least as much as you did before the new tax laws went into effect.

Now, with all of these changes in mind, it's time to make the proper financial moves. Then you, too, may become a winner.

(Materials provided by the Deloitte Haskins & Sells and the Grant Thornton accounting firms were used in compiling this chapter.)

4   Hottest Investments

The high-speed laser printers at the headquarters of Boston-based Fidelity Investments continue to spew out more than 200 million pages of investor transaction statements each month.

These statements tell the continuous story of major shifts by American mutual fund investors. For example, on one day following a record drop on Wall Street, cautious folks switched $285 million out of Fidelity stock mutual funds into its money market funds.

A recent visit to the offices of that fund giant and talks with managers who handle 72 different types of portfolios pointed out how sensitive this new world of investment really is, affected not only by new tax laws, but world markets and the day's headlines. The fund that is hot in one quarter or year may be a dog the next. Young fund managers vie for top billing on performance lists. It's survival of the fittest in a new climate in which the investor's money may be here one day, gone the next.

The visibility of the financial markets is incredibly high these days. The $100 million penalty slapped on financier Ivan Boesky by the Securities and Exchange Commission for insider trading violations and the subsequent far-reaching scandal was a worldwide cover story. Drawn into question were the insiders who profit from information regular investors don't hear about, the corporate raiders and those who finance the mega-buck takeover deals with low-quality "junk bond" issues.

With a general public so much more aware of investing's intrigues, it is no wonder that the packaged investments of today must have greater sophistication in their pitches.

Fund companies such as Fidelity, Vanguard Group, Dreyfus Corp., T. Rowe Price, Putnam Financial Services, American Capital Funds, Capital Research & Management, Kemper Financial and IDS Financial Services try to outperform each other in both returns and splashy advertising campaigns. Smaller investment firms work hard to find their performance niche as well. Firms pool investments such as stocks and bonds into individual funds with distinct goals, such as long-term growth, aggressive growth, high income or tax-free income. Investing is done by mail or telephone and switching money among a "family of funds" is frequently accomplished by simply picking up the telephone. Check-writing is available with many funds.

"It's too much work trying to follow individual stocks and I've been shifting out of them into mutual funds," one prosperous woman executive told me while waiting for a bill to be rung up in a department store recently. "I don't really care what the manager of the fund is up to, so long as the numbers show up on one of the year-end 'best fund return' lists." Not much to ask, eh? It's important to keep in mind that last year's performance doesn't assure anything, since changing trends determine which will do best. So look at long-term performance, the quality of the fund's managers and the quality of service the fund provides.

The new investments aren't just for people with the lifestyles of the rich and famous. Small investors with $1,000 or less to spend are no longer small potatoes in the eyes of the investment world, since many funds permit initial investment of $1,000 or less. In fact, Twentieth Century Investors, based in Kansas City, Mo., has no minimum investment requirement for six of its funds.

But whether you are looking at a fund, a unit trust, an annuity or a limited partnership, always watch the fees on today's fancily-packaged investments that can make a big dent in your return. About half of the mutual funds have what is called a front-end load, which is an initial sales charge that ranges anywhere from 2 to 9 percent. Most of these funds are sold through brokers or financial planners who receive part of that fee. Other funds have back-end loads deducted when you pull money out. No-load funds supposedly have no initial sales charge, though some have what's known as 12-b fees (named after a Securities and Exchange rule that permits them) in which sizable advertising credits or commissions are taken out as expenses each year you hold the fund. And, as we'll see later, a great many other types of investments sock it to the investor with added-on costs.

We'll also be taking a look at investing in stocks later, but clearly, the new investments packaged in shiny wrappers are the stars of modern investing that under the new tax laws Americans will choose to make money. Just make sure your choices take into account your individual tax bracket and your goals.

Winning long-term with stock funds

The superstar stock funds of the past 10 years didn't get that way by standing pat:

> — *The $6.7 billion-asset Fidelity Magellan Fund,* which has risen an amazing 1,616 percent in the past decade, is constantly changing its positions in the three categories—conservative stocks, growth companies and higher-risk cyclical issues. "During any market decline, I sell conservative stocks that tend to hold their price and buy stocks that have become reasonably priced but have potential," explained Peter

Lynch, the 42-year-old "wunderkind" who has managed that Boston-based fund to a top-ranked 297 percent gain for the five year period as well.

— *The $650 million Evergreen Fund,* up 910 percent over 10 years, has been buying shares of a small company called American Land Cruisers as one play on the new tax law. "People will be renting rather than buying recreational vehicles because they won't be able to deduct interest expenses under the new laws," reasoned Stephen Lieber, who manages that Harrison, N.Y.-based fund. "American Land Cruisers, which rents Winnebagos and the like, hopes to become the 'Hertz of the RVs'."

— *The $1.9 billion Twentieth Century Select Fund,* up 1,000 percent the past decade, is continuing the traditionally high turnover rate of its diversified portfolio. "Be patient and give the stock the time it needs, but keep that portfolio moving," said Robert C. Puff, portfolio manager for the no-load (no initial sales charge) fund in Kansas City, Mo. "While income-oriented stocks and bonds will benefit from tax reform, the basic investment goals of capital appreciation and compounding won't change."

Magellan, a load fund, has remained fully invested in the stock market the past decade, with little money in cash even during major downturns. Patience resulted in 20-fold gains in the stock of Zayre Corp. and the Service Corp. International funeral company. There have been 10-fold increases in Chrysler Corp. and the Pep Boys car-parts chain. "As a small fund, we were able to buy stocks of both small growth companies and big companies," noted Lynch, who oversees 1,400 different stocks. "But, at our current large asset size, it is obviously much more difficult to get the same dramatic results from small companies." Lynch has been expanding holdings in troubled utilities, drugs, electronics, food and beverages, trucking and energy. Twelve percent of holdings are in foreign stocks, down from 20 percent.

As far as the individual investor is concerned, Lynch believes it is always important to have clear logic behind any investment. "You should, for example, be able to explain to your daughter or son in several sentences why you hold a certain investment and what you expect it to do," he said.

Lieber, of the no-load Evergreen Fund, knows exactly what he expects of his investments. In emphasizing growth companies, his Evergreen has also profited from more than 160 takeovers "as many entrepreneurs decide to sell rather than hang in there to become the next Hewlett-Packard," he said. Its sister-fund, Evergreen Total Return, also no-load, is up 220 percent the past five years, helped by nearly 50 takeovers. Placing strong emphasis on convertible preferred stock and bonds, Nola Falcone, manager of Evergreen Total Return expects takeovers in grocery, utility and banking industries the next several years.

While you obviously must have short-term gains to get to long-term gains, these funds are in it for the long haul.

Some highly-specialized funds, particularly those that deal with only one sector such as technology or gold-mining, can give you a bumpy ride as their performance moves up or down dramatically with economic trends. They may have spectacular results in a given year, but aren't able to follow up. For most investors, switching around between sector funds is more trouble than they want with their investments. So a diversified fund whose philosophy is one they agree with is probably a better choice.

Latest star stock funds

In recent days, the nation's top-performing stock mutual has been counting heavily on the unpredictable airline industry to keep it flying high. Meanwhile, managers of most other highly rated funds were bowing gratefully to the East, pleased that they decided to send their investors' money to Japan.

"We're very bullish on the airline industry, with about 20

percent of our $6 million portfolio in airline stocks," said Kenneth Heebner, manager of the Zenith Fund. The fund, available through a New England Life variable life insurance policy, was up 85.01 percent in the first three quarters of 1986. Emphasizing capital appreciation for risk-oriented investors, Zenith has seen its stock in Texas Air Corp. double and has added stock of other airline firms such as AMR Corp. and NWA Corp.

Look down the list of stellar-performing funds the past couple of years and the emphasis, thanks to the weak dollar and booming overseas markets, is decidedly foreign. But, while prospects for Japanese growth and a weak U.S. dollar remain strong, overseas funds can't rely solely on those factors. So the funds are itching to expand into stocks of companies in countries such as South Korea, the Philippines and Taiwan once legal barriers are removed.

It's always worthwhile to peruse the lists of recent top performers to see whether your beliefs about what will be happening next fits in with their goals. The top mutual funds for the first three quarters of 1986, according to Lipper Analytical Services, were:

> — *Zenith Fund-Capital Growth*, offered through a New England Life variable life policy, managed by Loomis-Sayles & Co., Boston, up 85.01 percent.

> — *GT Pacific Growth Fund*, GT Global Growth Funds, San Francisco, no-load, up 75.71 percent.

> — *Merrill Lynch Pacific*, New York, load, up 70.19 percent.

> — *GT Japan Growth*, GT Global Growth Funds, San Francisco, no-load, up 69.68 percent.

> — *Fidelity Overseas*, Fidelity Investments, Boston, load, up 68.82 percent.

> — *BBK International*, available only to clients of Bailard Biel & Kaiser, San Mateo, Calif., $10,000 minimum investment, no-load, up 63.66 percent.

> — *Newport Far East*, Commonwealth Group, Richmond,

Va., no-load, redemption fee in first four years, up 62.34 percent.

— *Nomura Pacific Basin*, Securities International, New York, $20,000 minimum investment, no-load, up 61.94 percent.

— *Financial Portfolios-Pacific*, Financial Programs Inc., Englewood, Colo., no-load, up 60.68 percent.

— *Strong Opportunity*, Strong/Corneliuson Capital Management, Milwaukee, load, up 58.60 percent.

Tax-exempt municipals in the limelight

Now is the time to invest in tax-free municipal bonds. That's what investment companies around the nation have been urging in advertisements and personal calls to clients.

It's true that a lowering of tax brackets diminishes some of the advantage that municipals, which are free from federal tax, have held over taxable bonds. The higher one's bracket, the greater the relief such municipals offer.

But there are a great many positives to ponder. Tax-free municipals have been paying interest in some cases higher than taxable long-term government bonds, even before tax consequences are considered. Elimination of many other tax shelters makes municipals more attractive, and a reduced supply of bonds is expected to create greater demand.

Most public-purpose municipal bonds aren't touched by the new laws, noted one bond manager. Only private-purpose municipals sold to raise money for industrial projects will be taxable, and virtually all bonds issued before Jan. 1, 1986 will be "grandfathered in," so they'll retain tax-exempt status. In addition, he added, the current low rate of inflation makes municipal yields look particularly good.

Many fund families offer a variety of municipal bond funds tailored to the investor's demands in terms of yield and ability to cope with volatility of asset value. Funds with the highest

yields invest in long-term municipals that are the most volatile; funds investing in higher-quality long-term bonds receive
slightly less yield; and short-term bond funds and tax-exempt
money-market funds have considerably lower yield but little
price volatility.

Top-performing high-yield municipal bond funds for the
most recent 12-month period, according to Lipper, have been:

— *T. Rowe Price Tax-Free High Yield,* T. Rowe Price Associates, Baltimore, a no-load fund, recent yield 7.5
percent, total reinvested return (including price appreciation and reinvestment of dividends) up 18.56
percent.

— *Stein Roe High-Yield Municipals,* Stein Roe & Farnham, Chicago, no-load, recent yield 8 percent, total
return up 18.33 percent.

— *IDS High Yield Tax Exempt Fund,* IDS/American Express, Minneapolis, load, recent yield 8.9 percent,
total return up 18.2 percent.

— *Vanguard Muni High Yield Fund,* Vanguard Group,
Valley Forge, Pa., no-load, recent yield 8.1 percent,
total return up 17.88 percent.

— *Fidelity High Yield Municipals,* Fidelity Investments,
Boston, no-load, recent yield 7.9 percent, total return up 17.55 percent.

Fund managers say they're shifting their portfolios toward
lower-quality bonds to gain higher yields. Ten percent of one
typical fund was in issues below investment grade rating of
BBB, with 5 percent of that in issues that aren't rated at all by
agencies. With a fund, default of any one bond simply means
a decrease in overall yield, not the same disaster that befalls
one investor holding one bond in default. However, many individual bonds do carry insurance coverage, in exchange for
a slightly lower yield. In the future, funds will specialize in
specific types of bonds, such as state issues, in the same way
stock funds have specialized, one fund manager predicted.

Recently, investment firms have been pushing taxable municipal bonds as an investment, the initial sales being made to pension funds and big institutions, with individuals the next target. The investor should be aware that this is an entirely new market which—despite high yields, call protection (a guarantee against early redemption by the issuer) and generally high credit quality—could prove unpredictable. If an individual decides to sell before maturity, there may be wide ranges in prices offered in this new market. Detailed information on taxable municipals may also be hard to come by. In many cases, the bonds aren't pure obligations of government agencies but are instead secured by banks or insurance firms. The individual investor must decide whether some of the uncertainties are worth accepting in order to nail down an investment 1 to 2 percent higher in yield than Treasury bonds of similar duration.

Junk bond funds

Why do you think they call it junk?

That's a question to be pondered by American investors tossing record sums of money into high-yield, low-grade "junk" bond funds. The quality of bonds in such funds has been declining—at the very time assets have nearly doubled to $20 billion. Any investor must accept volatility.

Junk bonds are big money makers for Wall Street. Michael Milken of Drexel Burnham Lambert Inc., who was influential in popularizing junk bonds, made his debut on the Forbes magazine list of 400 richest Americans with a net worth of more than $500 million.

Featuring strong yields, junk bond funds look particularly good under tax reform's lower individual brackets. They'll be attracting even more investor dollars. "There certainly are delinquencies and bankruptcies, since those are the sort of companies that high-yield funds invest in," said one portfolio manager. "Quality of bonds overall is somewhat lower and riskier because more of them represent smaller companies carrying greater debt."

The industry-wide default rate on low-grade bonds is less than 2 percent, though some brokerage firms have logged considerably worse records with the bonds they've underwritten. The rationale behind investing in a fund is that it's made up of many bonds, thus blunting the possibility of major financial impact. IDS Extra Income, for example, has 60 percent of its portfolio in lower-grade bonds rated BB or below. Default in any one bond would simply mean a decrease in overall yield, not the big problem that befalls one investor holding one bond in default.

So the aggressive nature of the funds continues. "When the market was overreacting to the Chernobyl nuclear incident, we were busy buying bonds of Long Island Lighting and Consumers Power," said one portfolio manager. "While the typical investor with a certificate of deposit might not like a high-yield bond fund, these funds do have less volatility than stock funds." The LTV Corp. bankruptcy put the kibosh on high-yield funds and a considerable amount of money was withdrawn by investors, but they came back again. The fund strategy is that your home runs should offset your defaults.

When considering a junk bond fund, check out the diversity of its holdings and track record of the investment firm offering it. Junk bond funds have easily outperformed high-grade bond funds, but the quality of the individual fund manager really makes the biggest difference.

Top five taxable high-yield bond funds through the first nine months of 1986, according to Lipper, were:

— *IDS Extra Income Fund*, IDS Financial Services, Minneapolis, a load fund, recent yield 10.25 percent, up 15.49 percent in total reinvested return including price appreciation.

— *First Investors Special Bond Fund*, First Investors Management Co., New York, load, recent yield 11.40 percent, up 14.34 percent in total reinvested return.

— *Financial Bond Shares-High Yield Portfolio*, Financial Programs, Englewood, Colo., no-load, recent yield 11.2 percent, up 13.38 percent in total reinvested return.

— *Fidelity High Income Fund*, Boston, no-load, recent yield 11.2 percent, up 13.28 percent in total reinvested return.

— *Investment Portfolio-High Yield*, Kemper Investments, Chicago, no-load, recent yield 9.88 percent, up 13.24 percent in total reinvested return.

Ginnie Maes

Every time you think the Ginnie Mae is finally going down for the 10-count, that funny-sounding mortgage-backed investment finds some way or other to get back into the fight again.

Paying comparatively high yields, Ginnie Maes represent mortgages guaranteed by the U.S. government. Interest and principal are backed by the Government National Mortgage Association. They're expected to look even better under the new tax laws. "With so many other rates down, investors are turning to Ginnie Maes in large numbers once again," said Patrick Beimford, portfolio manager with Kemper U.S. Government Securities fund. "Tax reform should provide yet another boost, since a 9 percent return obviously looks far better in a 33 percent tax bracket than in a 50 percent bracket."

Assets of Ginnie Mae funds have grown in the past year by more than $13 billion to a total of $44 billion. Another three funds have made their debut along the way, bringing the current number to 26.

A fund that invests in Ginnie Maes is significantly different from a Ginnie Mae. The actual Ginnie Maes require hefty investment of $25,000. In addition, principal is usually paid back along with regular interest payments, so when you receive your final check you've nothing left.

Ginnie Mae mutual funds, on the other hand, invest in a

pool of Ginnie Maes and often permit investment of $1,000 or less. They typically allow check-writing. But, like any other investment, a Ginnie Mae is hardly perfect.

Ginnie Maes aren't as safe as some people think they are, and certainly not as risk-free as a money market fund or a Treasury bill. That's because, although backed by the government against default, the Ginnie Mae will fluctuate in value of assets and also yield. If interest rates decline, there's the risk of prepayment of mortgages in the pool by the nation's borrowers. That occurred in 1986 during the flood of mortgage refinancings, so investors got more cash back and less interest.

Some funds try to ease the worry by shying away from higher-yielding Ginnie Maes with the greatest risk of prepayment, though some others readily take the gamble to get high returns. "The investor simply must realize principal will fluctuate in value," said one product manager.

Top-performing mutual funds in the first nine months of 1986 that placed a minimum of 65 percent of portfolio in Ginnie Maes, according to Lipper, included:

- *Kemper U.S. Government Securities*, Chicago, a load fund, up 12.14 percent in total reinvested return, 9.85 percent recent yield.
- *Merrill Lynch Federal Securities Trust*, New York, load, up 9.94 percent in total reinvested return, 9.9 percent recent yield.
- *Decision Funds Government Income*, Alliance Capital Management Corp., New York, no-load, up 9.74 percent in total reinvested return, 9.33 percent recent yield.
- *Fidelity Ginnie Mae Portfolio*, Boston, no-load, up 8.87 percent in total reinvested return, 8.25 percent recent yield.

Tax-exempt and taxable money market funds

You can't keep a good fund down. The money market fund, that handy parking lot for investors who don't know where else to put their money, is growing in popularity again despite low yields.

A lot of those dollars are being parked in a type of money market fund that many investors don't even know exists. It's the tax-exempt, which has grown by $20 billion the past year to nearly $56 billion in assets. "A tax-exempt money market fund is basically a short-term municipal bond fund for an investor who wants liquidity without risk," explained one fund manager.

Such funds usually maintain a net asset value of $1 per share that seldom fluctuates. That makes them different from higher-yielding municipal bond funds that invest in longer-term instruments and often suffer dramatic swings in asset value. By investing in quality tax-free securities of one year or less, loss of principal is uncommon. For someone who sees most shelters disappearing under tax reform, tax-exempt money market funds provide a safe and liquid harbor.

While you pay for safety and liquidity with yields that were already low and have recently fallen even lower, those yields are exempt from federal tax. For a taxpayer in one of the higher levels of the new brackets, they'll remain attractive.

Most mutual fund families offer tax-exempt money markets. So, rather than split hairs over modest yields, many investors choose to place their money with the company in which they've already invested. After all, the dollars in money market funds are frequently shifted around to other types of funds eventually anyway.

Top tax-exempt money market funds in the most recent 12-month period, according to Lipper, were:

— *Financial Tax-Free Money Fund*, Financial Programs, Englewood, Colo., up 5.18 percent, recent yield 3.86 percent.

— *USAA Tax-Exempt Money Market fund*, USAA Investment Management Co., San Antonio, average yield 5.17 percent, recent yield 4.07 percent.

— *Calvert Tax-Free Reserves*, Calvert Group, Washington, D.C., average yield 5.11, recent yield 4.03 percent.

Traditional money market funds have fluctuated in overall assets from month to month, yet their assets still total $171 billion. A lot of money coming into the money markets is deposited when the stock market is having trouble. "Money market funds are more than a parking lot, however, since they offer higher yields than a bank and are cheaper than a checking account," said one fund manager.

Top money market mutual funds over the most recent 12-month period were:

— *Flex-Fund Money Market*, R. Meeder & Associates, Dublin, Ohio, average yield 7.29 percent, recent yield 5.61 percent.

— *U.S. Trust Master Money Fund*, U.S. Trust Co., New York (must have $10,000 in a combination of that firm's funds), average yield 7.27 percent, recent yield 5.9 percent.

— *Kemper Money Market Fund*, Kemper Financial, Chicago, average yield 7.25 percent, recent yield 5.46 percent.

With inflation under control, the real rate of return on money market funds is actually better than when yields were higher.

Convertible securities

Convertible securities have been on a roll, providing investors with solid growth while cushioning them from any sudden market drops. Already a favorite choice of cautious folks who want higher income than common stock and greater appreciation than regular bonds, convertibles look even better now. That's because their strong yields will benefit from tax reform's lower individual brackets.

By definition, convertibles are preferred stock or bonds exchangeable for a specified number of common shares at a set price. Perhaps the strongest selling point is that convertibles are not subject to the extremes that common stocks typically experience.

The investor receives interest, plus potential capital gain from stock appreciation realized when the bond is converted. While convertibles usually have a provision that gives the issuing firm a chance to call in the convertible at a specified price, it will never sell below its conversion value. For many investors, the biggest weakness of convertibles may be the callability, since you could conceivably lose something you'd really like to own.

Convertibles are being issued at a record rate of more than $12 billion a year. Because the recent performance of convertible securities has easily outstripped conventional stock, advertisements seem to be popping up everywhere. Investment firms are high on the prospect of a growing instrument that many folks don't yet understand. Primary advantage for the company issuing the convertible is that it makes the security more marketable.

E. F. Hutton & Co. was recently high on the convertible bonds of Control Data and Prime Motor Inns, while a favorite among convertible preferred stock was CIGNA Corp. The convertible should be thought of as a hedged sort of investment that usually doesn't rise as fast as a stock in a major market rise, but seldom has a negative return.

Mutual funds investing in convertible issues have grown in assets from $600 million to $1.6 billion in just the past year. Top-performing funds investing primarily in convertibles in the first three quarters of 1986, according to Lipper, were:

— *Dreyfus Convertible Securities*, Dreyfus Corp., New York, a no-load fund, total reinvested return up 22 percent.

— *Value Line Convertible*, Value Line Securities, New York no-load, up 21.21 percent.

— *Dean Witter Convertible*, Dean Witter Reynolds, New

York, no-load but requires redemption fee, up 19.29 percent.

— *American Capital Harbor*, American Capital Funds, Houston, a load fund, up 18.76 percent.

— *Putnam Convertible Income Growth*, Putnam Financial Services, Boston, a load fund, up 17.88 percent.

The convertible is particularly good for an individual retirement account, a retired person looking for income, or a pension plan. Fund managers caution, however, that not all returns may be as high in the future. That's because lower-quality companies are issuing convertibles and many other companies aren't offering quite as attractive terms. Dreyfus Convertible Securities fund has significant holdings in Cray Research convertible bonds. Value Line Convertible fund obtained its best results with the convertible bonds of Wal-Mart Stores, Fleet Financial and Triangle Industries.

Conscientious investing

South African violence over apartheid policies seems to have increased general investor desire to scrutinize ideology along with the bottom line. But there is, of course, no one party line on ethical investing. Criteria of each stock or money market fund with ethical goals varies, ranging from avoidance of tobacco or South Africa to actively seeking out equal employment or alternative energy sources.

"You must always narrow investment choices based on some sort of criteria anyway," explained one ethical fund manager. "So why not also include a company's record on equal employment, the environment and product safety, as well as its general reputation?" Many of the so-called "ethical" funds were begun in the early 1970's and acknowledge their appeal to investors from a Woodstock generation grown into upwardly mobile adults.

Calvert Social Investment Managed Growth, Washington,

D.C., a load fund, won't invest in companies with nuclear or defense interests or that operate in South Africa. It has had an annual return of about 17 percent over the past three years. Dreyfus Third Century, New York, no-load, chooses companies that conserve natural resources and emphasize employee safety. It has averaged about a 10 percent return each of the past three years.

Pax World, Portsmouth, N.H., no-load, doesn't invest in military-tied, alcohol, tobacco or gambling companies. It is up 17 percent in annual return the past three years. Pioneer Group, Boston, offers several funds, none of which put money in companies involved in alcohol or gambling or that have interests in South Africa. Other smaller funds with ethical goals include the New Alternatives Fund of Great Neck, N.Y., and the Parnassus Fund of San Francisco.

Telephone switching

Aggressive personalities may be best suited to the "telephone switch" strategy for mutual funds. Confident that they can spot trends, these investors quickly transfer money from one mutual fund to another when they sense changing market conditions.

In most cases, only a telephone call is required to make the switch happen, particularly with firms that feature a large family of funds. Dozens of mutual funds newsletters recommend switch timing. Their goal: to help subscribers buy into funds at their low points and sell at high points. Money is moved in and out of funds of different stock groups, or into money market funds. It can be a tricky business. The newsletter editors who plot switch timing say their clients benefit more from their advice in a "down" market than in an "up" one.

"I make recommendations to invest in specific funds when they're down in value, so big profits can be made as they come back," explained Peter Eliades, publisher of the Los Angeles-based Stockmarket Cycles newsletter.

Charles Hooper, editor of the Mutual Fund Strategist newsletter in Burlington, Vt., comes up with model investment portfolios that invest equal parts in a variety of funds. For example, he has separate suggested portfolios for big companies such as Fidelity and Vanguard. When conditions change, the mutual fund newsletter editors recommend changing the mix.

Keep in mind that some mutual fund companies limit the number of switches they permit to three to four a year. Others have exit fees from certain funds. A few companies stopped switches altogether, because newsletter recommendations caused major gyrations in their portfolios. If you intend to switch around, make sure you know all the restrictions of the particular mutual fund company you're investing with.

Unit trusts

Middle-aged investors are getting some respect. They're the primary target of a barrage of seminars, mailings, advertisements and telephone calls aimed at selling municipal-bond unit trusts, which yield tax-free interest.

These neatly packaged but strange-sounding investments allow folks with conservative goals and a willingness to tie up their money for the long term to invest as little as $1,000 in a diversified package of municipals. Yields are high when compared with taxable issues. Many unit trusts offer private insurance coverage, which cuts the yield by a fraction but soothes the nerves of investors more accustomed to bank certificates than Wall Street. There's no continuing management fee because bonds cannot be added to the portfolio once it has been put together. The investor can get monthly checks and full principal back at maturity.

However, no matter what sales pitch you may receive, unit trusts aren't for everyone. The people interested are those who realize they don't have many more years of work to recover money they might lose on adventuresome investments.

They are designed for people who simply buy and hold. An experienced investor with more than $10,000 could invest in individual municipal bonds more cheaply because of lower commissions. An investor unsure how long he wants to commit his money would be better off with a municipal-bond mutual fund that permits him to shift out easily. So unit trusts are really for people who have determined what interest rates are going to do over the next few years and are confident about locking in a return.

Unit trusts aren't cheap. They usually require a hefty initial commission of 4.5 percent or more, and companies putting them together often charge more for the units than they did for the bonds they represent. You may have to commit to a trust for 25 to 30 years, rather than 10 years, to get a top rate. If you wish to sell your trust on the secondary market before it matures and prevailing rates are higher than when you bought, your principal will take a beating.

These big moneymakers for investment firms are gaining popularity, growing in the last decade from a market of $1 billion to more than $15 billion, largely because of the changing psychology of consumers. "We find that investors now want a package product in which they don't have to make selections or deal with volatility," said John N. Daly, who heads the unit-trust department of New York's Salomon Brothers investment banking firm. "A unit trust is safe, convenient, has good yield and permits you to either live off its income or reinvest it until retirement." Salomon Brothers' Johnny-come-lately entry into the unit-trust market to do battle with established leaders such as John Nuveen & Co. of Chicago, Van Kampen Merritt & Co. of Naperville, Ill., and Merrill Lynch & Co. indicates the amount of money to be made in unit trusts. Other firms are in the wings, ready to roll.

Keep in mind that, while actively managed mutual funds can easily outperform trusts in an up market, the trust may make up for it in down markets.

There are a number of different types of unit trusts, even

though those employing municipal bonds are the most popular. For example, many Americans who want to take the plunge into the high-flying stock market are understandably afraid that they'll wind up losing some of their initial investment. Two hybrid unit trusts, the Kemper Double Play Trust and the PaineWebber Pathfinders Trust, let you invest in the stock market with a guarantee that you won't lose any of your initial principal.

Kemper Double Play Trust combines investment in "zero-coupon" U.S. Treasury bonds (deeply discounted instruments with a final guaranteed payout) with an aggressive stock mutual fund. Minimum investment is $5,000, or $250 for individual retirement accounts. Fifty percent of the trust's assets are being invested in zero coupons and 45 percent in Kemper Summit Fund. There is a 5 percent sales charge and an annual management fee. The zero coupons will double in price by the time they mature. The worst that can happen if you hold the investment until maturity is getting back your initial investment. Of course, a savvy investor could diversify on his own as effectively with several investments without shelling out the commission for this unique package. Meanwhile, PaineWebber Pathfinders Trust has a $1,000 minimum and 4.5 percent sales commission and invests in zero coupons and stocks. Basically the same stocks remain in the trust for its duration, so there is no annual management fee.

Investing in bonds

Bonds are once again looking good to individual investors in search of steady interest income. First-time investors should realize, however, that shifts in inflation and interest rates can make the value of a bond every bit as volatile as the price of a stock. Just ask an experienced bond investor who was burned by the high inflation and rates of the 1970's.

Bond investors must be willing to accept volatility. For example, the Salomon Brothers investment firm calculates that the high inflation of 1979 contributed to long-term quality corporate bonds declining 4 percent in total return, which included price changes. Conversely, in less-inflationary 1982, total return from corporate bonds jumped 40 percent from the year before.

Bonds work best with a "buy-and-hold" philosophy. The goal is to receive interest along the way to getting your money back at maturity. Intermediate bonds of high quality are still the most popular for individuals. There's a higher risk of default with higher yielding bonds rated "BB plus" or lower by Standard & Poor's.

U.S. Treasury notes and bonds are the best bet for safety, though you can obtain a higher yield with corporate bonds. Municipal bonds free from federal tax can offer an even better deal, depending on your individual tax bracket. For those who prefer investing a smaller amount and who seek diversity, there are the bond mutual funds and unit trusts. "For a long time, the bond market was dominated by big institutions, but more individuals are investing these days," said one broker who specializes in bonds. "While it's possible to buy individual bonds in denominations of $1,000, nearly all transactions are $5,000 or more."

New investors should keep in mind that the most corporate and municipal bonds have "call" features, which specify a time at which the issuer can retire the security early and pay off bondholders. Bonds are usually called when interest rates fall so significantly that the issuer can save money by floating new bonds at lower rates. Many bonds have been called the past several years. It is vitally important that an investor be aware of the call date. After all, if you're expecting to get interest for 10 years and the bond is called in two years, you're certainly not getting what you had wanted.

Zero-coupon bonds

As soon as President Reagan signed the new tax laws, big Wall Street investment houses were rushing to market with millions of dollars of a newly-authorized investment known as a stripped municipal bond. Stripped municipals separate the interest payments on the bonds from principal payments so that each becomes a separate zero-coupon security.

As we explained earlier, the popular zero-coupon securities don't pay interest, but are sold at a deep discount in a concept similar to U.S. savings bonds. The investor's return comes from the difference between the discounted price and face value at maturity.

The new stripped municipals are designed to adapt to changes under the new tax laws which limit a parent's ability to shelter income through gifts to children. Through these new instruments, parents can put the money in investments exempt from federal tax for one to eight or nine years in anticipation of a child's education costs. That's not as long a time-period as most zero-coupon municipals, which are 10 years or longer in duration and require significant advance planning. These new instruments can also be used in retirement planning.

So times have certainly changed. Zero-coupon bonds, those "sure-thing" investments offering a set final payout, are no longer just for individual retirement accounts as they were a short time ago. Banks have joined brokerage firms in touting the benefits of zero coupons, helping to push the total amount invested to more than $100 billion. Unfortunately, increased popularity hasn't altered the fact that many investors don't understand the basic problems in selling zero-coupon bonds before maturity, their tax liability and the commission charges.

The obvious selling point of these deeply discounted instruments, ranging in duration from six months to 30 years, is that they feature a final face value. It's a predictable concept similar to U.S. savings bonds. Each bond will be worth exactly $1,000 at maturity. Such zero-coupon bonds packaged by brokerage firms are sold under a confusing array of Treasury-based acronyms such as CATS, TIGRS and TRs at various firms. Heavily promoted by both banks and brokerage firms, STRIPS (Separate Trading of Registered Interest and Principal of Securities) are direct Treasury obligations. Other choices include zero certificates of deposit, corporate zeroes, government mortgage-based zeroes and municipal zeroes.

Once an investor sorts through the variations, there are still complications. "I don't think a lot of investors are fully aware that zero-coupon bonds are the most volatile bonds of all if you need to sell them," warned one portfolio manager. Should you decide to sell your zero on the secondary market before maturity and interest rates are up, it won't be worth as much. So only invest to buy and hold.

Consider the tax implications. Taxable zero coupons require that you pay tax on your interest annually, even though you don't actually receive that interest until maturity. Commission charges can significantly cut your yield. One class-action suit claimed that a major brokerage firm did not disclose the actual net yield on zero-coupon bonds. Yield was less than expected because of hefty commissions.

Net yield is what's important and should be stated on your order's confirmation statement, according to Securities and Exchange Commission officials. But one must carefully shop those yields in the first place with the commission in mind. That's because after-commission yields and maturities can vary significantly among institutions. In addition, some firms bill their fees separately. Always question the person selling you the bond about all costs before you purchase, since it is not unusual to be misled.

Savings bonds

Though U.S. savings bonds have traditionally offered all the sex appeal of receiving a sensible shirt on your birthday, they've made a comeback. Sales have gained significantly in the 1980s, propelled by a new competitive formula for setting their interest.

There was an all-out savings bond rush in the months prior to the Treasury Department's cut on Nov. 1, 1986 of the guaranteed minimum for new bonds held five years. That minimum guarantee went from 7.5 percent to 6 percent, along with the government's added assertion that "periodic changes up or down in the minimum rate on new bonds are likely in the future."

While it made them a bit less attractive, that move didn't kill savings bonds. Remember that semi-annual rates based on 85 percent of five-year Treasury securities yields are announced each May and November. For each period, the interest rate received will vary. So if you hold your new bond five years and the accumulated market-based rates are higher than the guaranteed minimum payout, you'll get that higher return instead.

Under the new tax laws, U.S. savings bonds still make sense for anyone putting money aside for their children or seeking extreme safety in investments. The fact that the investor can postpone paying tax on the interest still makes them appealing, although they should only be a portion of an overall personal portfolio. Because the new tax laws do away with income-shifting techniques by taxing virtually all of a child's income at the parent's rate until age 14, savings bonds provide a new strategy. Buy savings bonds in the child's name using his Social Security number, with the intent of redeeming them after he reaches age 14, financial planners counsel. At that cash-in point, the accumulated interest will be taxed at the child's lower tax bracket.

The same is true for a high-income adult approaching retirement in several years, who can buy savings bonds now and redeem them in a lower tax bracket after retirement.

Some financial planners agree that the tax-deferred, government-guaranteed aspects of savings bonds make them fine for socking away smaller amounts of money, but believe there are other investment choices that do similar things. "There are many investments with higher yields, safety and tax deferral, such as tax-deferred annuities, though you won't have quite the same guarantees as the government," noted one planner.

The new Series EE bonds have a maturity period of 12 years.

As before, EE bonds are exempt from state and local taxes, and federal tax may be deferred until a bond is redeemed or reaches final maturity. Denominations range from a $50 bond that can be bought for $25 to a $10,000 bond costing $5,000. In between there are $75, $100, $200, $500 and $1,000 denominations, all available at half that face value.

If the market-based rate applying to a bond is higher than the current minimum, it will double in value sooner and continue to earn interest to maturity. Bonds held less than five years earn interest at lower rates which are fixed and graduated, depending on how long they're held. The rate paid on bonds held six months, for example, is 4.16 percent, while the rate for those cashed in after three years would be 5.01 percent.

An investor can still postpone paying taxes on the bond by cashing it in and purchasing what's called a Series HH bond at the same time. The rate on new issues of HH bonds has been cut to a flat 6 percent over a 10-year period. Interest on both H and HH bonds is paid semiannually by check. (Remember that EE bonds purchased before Nov. 1, 1986 as well as all Series E bonds and savings notes eligible for market-based interest retain a 7.5 percent minimum rate through their original or extended maturity.)

Savings bonds are big business. A total of $86 billion in savings bonds is outstanding, including about $25 billion of Series EE bonds, which were first offered in 1980.

Treasury securities

If it's safety you want, Treasury bills backed by the U.S. government certainly have it. Bills are sold in denominations of $10,000 in three-, six- and 12-month maturities. Notes are generally sold in minimums of $5,000 when their maturity is less than four years and $1,000 when the maturity is longer than that. Maturities range from one to 10 years. Meanwhile, treasury bonds sell in $1,000 minimums and have maturities longer than 10 years. While their yield is a percentage point or so lower than the issues of top corporations, their safety is unsurpassed. You can buy Treasury issues through any of the dozen Federal Reserve banks, 25 branch offices or by mail using forms obtained from your local Federal Reserve bank.

Tax shelters

Tax shelters have felt the wrath of the new tax laws. Often requiring a significant commission charge and a degree of risk, limited partnerships basically permit investors to buy a portion of a pooled business venture with underlying investments such as shopping malls, apartment buildings, cable television stations, movie projects or oil wells. They usually provide some income along the way to a final payout when the investment has run its course and is sold in several years.

The prior goal of tax losses has been replaced by income-generation for the vast majority of partnerships, a move already in motion and only accelerated by the new laws. Everything is being bought with cash and little debt. That's because lower tax rates reduce the value of many tax breaks and the new laws also limit the investor's ability to use tax shelter losses to reduce ordinary taxable income.

As explained in the chapter on specifics of the new laws, losses from passive investments in which the taxpayer does not materially participate (limited partnerships and most rental real estate) will be partly deductible against nonpassive income on a gradually declining scale until 1991. The remaining losses will be deductible only against passive income, and most shelter owners don't have much in the way of passive income. Syndicators of some existing partnerships are attempting to help out their investors by renegotiating the financing on deals already in effect to include more income and less debt.

It may be a better idea for someone currently holding an outmoded tax shelter to look around for limited partnerships that will generate passive income to deduct the passive losses against, for there are plenty of these being offered. There are also some specialized investment companies that actually buy up existing partnership interests, among them, Liquidity Fund Investment Corp., Emeryville, Calif., and Equity Resources Group, Cambridge, Mass. Unfortunately, you won't be in much of a position to demand the best price possible for your holdings.

As a special deal in the new tax laws for the troubled energy industry, losses from oil and gas wells in which an investor has a "working interest" can still be deducted against active and portfolio income, though this also means accepting un- limited liability. Considering the risk and the lower tax brack- ets under the new tax laws, many experts think it isn't worth the effort.

New investors should always make sure they aren't buying an old type of shelter renamed or repackaged to make it look like one of the new income-producing partnerships.

The basic shift toward income-producing shelters was well underway before the new tax laws hit. A few years ago, 70 percent of partnerships offered by E. F. Hutton & Co. were designed to generate tax losses, but that percentage began to dwindle on the way to evaporating. "The shelter concept be- gan to die in the late 1970s, when the IRS acted like it was on a mission from God and really tightened the screws," said one executive who specializes in partnerships. "The new tax laws underscore the transformation of the business already underway."

An ideal example of the new trend is the Merrill Lynch & Co., ML Media Partners limited partnership offered last year. For a $5,000 minimum, investors were given the chance to share in profits from buying and selling smaller television, ca- ble, radio and magazine properties. "We're looking at every variety of business for partnerships these days, though the entertainment business and cable systems are getting a major push," said William Turchyn, an E. F. Hutton senior vice pres- ident whose own company's Silver Screen II partnership offered a crack at financing films produced by Walt Disney Productions.

There certainly is risk, for there are really no guarantees whatsoever in most of these investments as far as dividend return or final payout. Most set qualifying standards in their prospectuses as to what types of investors should be capable of assuming such chances. Frequently, significant fees are exacted by the sponsor, sometimes as high as 10 to 20 percent of the investor's initial outlay. They also can't offer what they once did. Shearson Lehman Brothers' Prime Cable Income partnership bears this warning to investors in its prospectus to let everyone know times have changed: "This partnership does not offer tax benefits commonly associated with tax shelter investments. Purchasers seeking substantial tax deductions should find alternative investments."

Real estate limited partnerships are being constructed with cash rather than debt, since tax revision lengthens the depreciable life of real estate and reduces tax benefits available in any one year.

Returns from partnerships, which often require no more than $1,000 to $5,000 for initial investment, can run from 7 percent to better than 15 percent, say syndicators, though each partnership is unique. Read the prospectus to find the degree of risk. Know what the underlying properties are in the partnership, whether they be films or apartment buildings. Remember that these investments tie up your money for as long as six or seven years and early exit can take a big bite out of the investment because there is only a small secondary market. Always check commissions and fees, as well as logic behind the investment and track record of those running it. The quality of the investment company and the managers of the partnership are the most important considerations.

While the shift is on to income-oriented partnerships based on the economic fundamentals rather than tax benefits, they should be viewed as a means of diversification beyond an individual portfolio of stocks and bonds. They are clearly not like money in the bank.

Real estate investment trusts and master limited partnerships

Some portions of the real estate industry do much better than others under the new tax laws. Real estate investment trusts (REITs) are publicly-traded and manage a portfolio of real estate to earn profits for shareholders. They are exempt from paying taxes on either income or gains passed on to their investors, as long as they meet a series of tests set out in the tax code. One requirement is that 95 percent of income must be distributed to shareholders. REITs will no longer be competing against tax-shelter syndications and there is now also greater flexibility in their management and operations.

Publicly-traded master limited partnerhsips (MLPs) also come out ahead under the new tax laws. They combine real estate investments designed for tax shelter with those that provide income to benefit the investor. MLPs escape the double taxation that hits companies, in that only distributions paid to unit holders are likely taxable but not earnings at the partnership level. So-called "roll-out" MLPs, for example, have been used by corporations to spin off real estate assets. Compared to REITs, MLPs aren't as limited in the types of investments they can make and are also able to pass tax losses through to investors. Their income is considered passive in the new tax laws and can be offset by passive losses from existing tax shelters, while REIT dividends are portfolio income that cannot be used to offset passive losses fully.

Commodity funds

As a youngster, long before "triple-witching" days or computerized trading became topics of concern to investors or the Securities and Exchange Commission, I took a field trip to one of the Chicago exchanges. My teacher had explained to our class that we'd learn that day what free enterprise was all about. About 20 minutes into observing the brightly jacketed traders in the frenzied "pits" shout at the top of their lungs, make animated but inscrutable hand gestures, and run around at full speed, I turned anxiously to my pal Rick.

"Free enterprise is in deep, deep trouble," I whispered, hoping few other unsuspecting Americans had witnessed the unsettling sight.

There really is a method to the seeming madness of commodity futures, the trading in contracts to buy or sell an amount of a commodity or financial instrument at a set price on a future date. These days even smaller investors can play this high-risk futures game through nearly 100 public funds with initial investments as low as $5,000, or $2,000 for individual retirement accounts. Funds pool money to invest in stock index futures, interest rate futures, currencies, precious metals or a variety of conventional commodities. The pool usually liquidates if more than half the capital is lost in the market.

After floundering much of the 1980s, commodity funds are making a comeback because of rising commodity prices and volatility in financial markets. While some funds have acknowledged losing big, the average fund is up 8 percent and some better than 40 percent. Meanwhile, assets have mushroomed in the last decade from $15 million to more than $700 million.

Should you decide to risk investing, keep only a small part of your overall portfolio in these funds—just to be on the safe side. Many require hefty front-end load (sales charge) of 8 percent or more, as well as commissions of more than 10 percent a trade. "Funds that have recently done best are broadly diversified, so the manager has more to do with success rather than any one commodity does," explained Morton S. Baratz, editor of *Managed Account Reports*, Columbia, Md., which tracks the funds. "Trading in interest rate futures, Treasury bills and foreign currencies have all provided good performance."

Another fund tracker, Jay Klopfenstein, president of Norwood Securities in Chicago, says the typical investor has "a speculative bent." He might be someone who tried unsuccessfully to trade on his own, or who knows little about commodities but wants a shot at a hedge or gain.

Managers said proudly that they make their moves based on technical factors, not the economy. The most successful manager in 1986, Dinesh Desai of Desai & Co., invested in markets such as coffee, grain, financial futures and crude oil. "We love volatility and days like the one in which the stock market took a big plunge, for being on the right side of moving markets is what makes us money" Desai asserted. "A stagnant market in any commodity, such as grain has experienced recently, means there's no opportunity for us to make money."

Top-ranking commodity funds in the first three quarters of 1986 based on after-commission performance, according to *Managed Account Reports*, were:

- *McCormick I*, front-end load, Desai & Co., Mountain View, Calif., up 59.1 percent.
- *Trendview Commodity VI*, Desai, no-load, up 53 percent.
- *Boston Futures Fund III* (now closed to new investors), Colorado Commodities Management, St. Paul, Minn., up 51.2 percent.
- *McCormick Fund III*, Desai & Co., front-end load, up 50.5 percent.
- *North American Commodity Fund I*, Desai, front-end load, up 49.1 percent.
- *Trendview Commodity Fund IV*, Desai, no-load, up 48.3 percent.
- *Thomson Financial Futures I*, Christopher Funk & Co., and Campbell & Co., Lafayette, Ind., front-end load, up 42.7 percent.
- *Palo Alto Futures Fund*, Desai, front-end load, up 42 percent.
- *Thomson Financial Futures II*, Christopher Funk & Co., front-end load, up 38.7 percent.

The hot ones

Number one with a bullet. The two hottest groups of investments moving up the Wall Street charts in recent days have all the flash and packaging of an album from a modern rock band.

Catching the fancy of fickle American investors have been:

—A wide variety of new stock issues that, in some cases, have featured spectacular results. Home Shopping Network, initially offered to the public at $18 a share last May, shot to $133 before settling back down a bit and then splitting. Other new stocks sporting high-tech names such as ATI Medical, Digitext and Enviropact gained more than 100 percent in price the year they were offered.

—Closed-end mutual funds introduced by high-profile investment personalities such as Marty Zweig, Charles Allmon and Mario Gabelli. All sold out quickly. A closed-end fund pools money from many investors to buy equities, but, unlike a typical mutual fund, has a fixed number of shares that trade on exchanges just like a conventional stock. Zweig Fund, Allmon's Growth Stock Outlook and Gabelli Equity Trust are traded on the New York Stock Exchange, and more such closed-end funds are on the way.

Though back in style this year, the new issues market is familiar to many investors—some of them losers in the past with this volatile and risky game. Big institutions and the customers of the brokerage firm underwriting the new issue usually get first crack at them, though individuals can try to keep up with them through their broker or by subscribing to specialized newsletters.

For example, the newsletter "New Issues: The Investor's Guide to Initial Public Offerings," in late 1986 was recommending an upcoming offering of 6.5 million shares of Carolco Pictures by PaineWebber Inc. and several other brokerage firms. That company was formed by the producers of the two "Rambo" movies that starred Sylvester Stallone. It had plans for several big-budget films annually, some tentatively with Stallone. The newsletter based at 3471 N. Federal Hwy., Ft. Lauderdale, Fla. 33306, depicted these shares as "short-term, high-risk, speculative holding." Another of its selections was WTD Industries, an aggressive lumber producer whose offering was made through the Piper, Jaffray & Hopwood brokerage firm.

View any new issue as high-risk, some of them having plenty of kick right after the initial offering and then taking a tumble. In this book's chapter on investing in stocks, the pitfalls, of new issues and the so-called "penny stock" market will be considered.

"There are some skyrockets, but most wind up losers that just sit there and erode in price," warned John B. Hoffmann, manager of equity research for Smith Barney, Harris Upham & Co. "However, one our firm brought out, the Toll Brothers home-building company, came out at $12, moved up more than three dollars right away and is still recommended because it's cheap."

Closed-end funds have also been around a long time, but in 1986 alone more than 20 new funds were issued with assets exceeding $4 billion. Because the investments are sold as shares on an exchange, they permit smaller investors to benefit from big-time money managers without an enormous initial investment. Since funds are fixed in their amount of capital, managers such as Zweig, Allmon and Gabelli can structure portfolios exactly as they want without worrying about money coming into the fund or redemptions. If the fund has been out a while, check its peformance against the market, but if it's new, you must rely on the track record and philosophy of the manager.

Some experts don't like investing in the newest closed-end funds. "Stay away from new funds, since they sell at a premium so the underwriter makes his money," said Thomas J. Herzfeld, a broker who specializes in closed-end funds and publishes the Closed-End Fund Monthly Update, 7800 Red Rd., South Miami, Fla. 33143. "Avoid it when it's new, then buy shares a bit later when they're selling at somewhat of a discount." A closed-end fund is a good deal when its shares sell at a discount to net asset value. Herzfeld was recently recommending shares of Scandinavia Fund (American Stock Exchange), France Fund (New York Stock Exchange), First Financial Fund (NYSE) and Baker, Fentress & Co. (over the counter). However, discounts and trends change, so be sure you've updated yourself on the progress of such a fund before investing.

5   All That Glitters

The American investor still loves the romance of collectibles. They spur the imagination with dreams of riches. But only in select cases and with thoughtful planning do they really have a positive effect on anyone's pocketbook. Most are meant to be bought and held, and their value as inflation hedges must take into account hard-to-predict factors such as world economic events.

The debut of the American Gold Eagle, America's new gold coin, was such a success that its first offering was quickly snapped up. The West Point Depository where the coins are minted began working seven-day-a-week shifts to keep up with demand. Most of the orders were small ones from average folks seeking a bit of glitter, perhaps as a gift to children. In addition, the Eagle has also been approved by the government to be put in individual retirement accounts.

High-quality diamonds have increased in price in recent months, but still carry much lower price tags than during the inflationary 1970s. Though prices may go up further, buy for love, not investment.

A neighbor of mine always used to point with pride to the long row of collector plates that dominated her living room wall. She'd tell her children with pride: "Someday, these will

all be yours and you'll thank me!" Her children were somewhat surprised to find that buyers were hardly beating down
the door when they later tried to sell those gaudy plates that
they inherited.

When I was a youngster, my pal Mike compiled a large collection of comic books featuring the superheroes of the time.
He kept them for safekeeping in a closet, pointing out that
they would be worth a pretty penny one day. Some years later
I asked Mike about some of those hard-to-find comics and he
didn't seem interested in talking about them. After some prod-
ding, he finally explained: "Well, my mom's cat sort of, well,
relieved himself on them and they aren't worth much anymore in the condition they're in."

Or consider the artwork purchased at one of those fancy
walk-in high-pressure galleries on the major boulevards in
many cities. During one brief stop-in I made with a friend, a
salesperson pointed to a hideous red-and-black watercolor that
should have been titled *Sailboating with Darth Vader*. I laughed.
The salesperson scowled. He said: "This is an investment offered through a special deal with our chain of galleries. It will
grow on you." (Doesn't every American need an expensive
painting that he hates?)

Collectibles feature a lot of variables that make it necessary
to "bone up" on information about whatever specialty strikes
your particular fancy.

One of my most vivid financial recollections is a visit to
inspect the gold reserves vault beneath the New York Federal
Reserve Bank. As you exit the elevator, there's a very dingy
hallway that promises little. But beyond that door—and
through some very tight security—is much of the world's gold
supply. Big bars of gold are tended by workmen in steel-toed
boots (dropping one of those massive gold bars can obliterate
a foot). Gold, whether in bars or coins, retains an allure that
hails back to the days when kingdoms waged battles over it.

Some Americans love to wear gold, while others collect it
as coins and quite a few dabble in gold-mining stocks or mutual funds. Most any dealer can relate instances of sober inves-

tors buying gold bullion with the intent of keeping it under their mattress or buried in the backyard—just in case the world economic system falls apart.

Primarily considered a hedge against inflation, gold disappointed investors with a plunge from its high of $875 an ounce in 1980. After spending time below $300 an ounce, it moved beyond $400 in 1986 due to social unrest in South Africa, where 60 percent of the world's gold supply is mined. Its road is always a bumpy one, yet its schizophrenic track record doesn't deter the true believers. "Gold was money 2,000 years ago and will still be money in another 2,000 years," as one portfolio manager for a gold fund told me. Gold should never comprise more than 5 to 10 percent of an individual's portfolio, since it is volatile.

The Treasury Department struck the first new gold coin since 1933 in the fall of 1986. The American Gold Eagle coins come in four weights, their prices tied to the spot quote for gold. The $50 face-value coin contains one troy ounce of gold; $25, one-half ounce; $10, one-quarter ounce; and $5, one-tenth ounce. The face value makes each coin "legal tender," though the coins won't go into circulation so long as gold values far outstrip face value. (Gold in late 1986 was selling at just under $400 an ounce.) The price you pay for the coin depends on the price of gold on the day you buy, plus a premium of 6 to 10 percent charged by the dealer or bank.

It pays to shop around, since some dealers that advertise heavily tend to jack up their premiums. Uncle Sam does not set the price on the coins as some people may mistakenly believe. Look for the best price you can find, and don't be surprised if there is a wide variety of prices. While the smaller coins cost less, the premium you pay will likely be higher.

The dealer you bought the coins from will also buy them back, but the amount you receive will depend on the value of gold at the time you sell. An investor is better off buying a one-ounce coin rather than a bar of precious metal because it can be sold more easily and won't require assaying of its content. The investor can also buy certificates that represent an actual holding in the metal. It is also better to buy a nation's coin that is in great supply, making it easier to sell.

Americans have been spending more than $1 billion a year on foreign gold coins, and the U.S. wants to keep that money at home. When the U.S. banned import of the South African Krugerrand, the Canadian Maple Leaf quickly filled the void as the best-selling gold coin, with the Chinese Panda, best known for its use in jewelry, also picking up quite a bit. The Maple Leafs are 99.9 percent fine gold; Krugerrands are 91.67 percent fine gold and 8.33 percent copper; and the U.S. Eagles are 91.67 percent gold, three percent silver and 5.33 percent copper. The U.S mixed in silver and copper in order to have a better-looking gold color and bigger coin.

The market for platinum, available in bars or in the Noble coin from Great Britain, is volatile, with run-ups of several hundred percent in price experienced in the mid-1980's as it shot past to $700 an ounce, then stumbled. Platinum is used in automobile catalytic converters and other industrial purposes. The Japanese have been heavy buyers of platinum for use in jewelry. South Africa produces more than 80 percent of the world platinum supply.

Silver, well-known for the Hunt family of Texas trying in vain to corner the market, has been in the doldrums compared to platinum and gold, its value hurt by cut-backs in its use in photographic applications. It can be pulled upward by movements in those other metals, but collecting silver in bars can be a problem. It takes quite a load of silver to equal the value of gold or platinum, so hauling around or storing your investment is difficult. "We find investors coming in to order silver, expecting to pick it up in a brown paper bag and carry it home in their pocket," laughed one metals dealer. "You should see their faces when they try to pick up that heavy, heavy bag."

In the midst of all the hubbub over the U.S gold coins, the companion silver bullion dollar didn't get as much publicity. Yet the U.S. Silver Eagle, a 99.9 percent pure one ounce silver bullion dollar, was a sell-out when initially offered in late November 1986. It was selling at about $2 over the market value of silver, or about $7.50, in late 1986. While the performance of silver prices has hardly been dramatic, it offers an inexpensive way to get involved in collecting precious metals. Coin dealers hope it will help boost the price of silver in the future.

Because of the decline in interest rates, argue the precious metals dealers, holding precious metals isn't expensive for the investor because he's not missing out on a strong return elsewhere. Although inflation is expected to rise only modestly near-term, its growth does fuel interest in precious metals. Always store precious metals in a safe place, such as a bank safe deposit box.

Buying stock in gold-mining companies is another way to play the precious metals market, since these stocks generally follow the rise and fall of metals prices. With a Nevada gold mine producing 220,000 ounces of gold annually, Battle Mountain Gold is a North American stock often recommended by gold-mining analysts. North American gold-mining stocks typically rise in price whenever turmoil in South Africa threatens to affect the mines of that nation. There are more than 20 gold-oriented mutual funds, among them USAA Gold Fund, a no-load fund based in San Antonio, Tex., with no South African investments; and Freedom Gold & Government Fund, a load fund run by Tucker Anthony & R.L. Day in Boston, also with no South African investments.

Gold and silver medallions minted by private companies became popular in the 1970s when gold was benefitting from rising prices. It is estimated that only one out of 10 such commemorative items can be sold for more than the meltdown value of the metal itself. Unless you're willing to go to great lengths to carefully seek out a good bet or have confidence in an expert, it's really not worth bothering with such collectibles.

While hardly as time-honored as gold investments, speculation in the latest baseball cards and comic books is also alive and well in the 1980s.

Some collectors are interested also in hard-to-find older examples that might be collecting dust in your family closet. Most aren't worth much or aren't in good enough condition to command a decent price even if they are rare. Wheeling and dealing in recent years has been done by speculators buying up large quantities of baseball cards depicting Dwight Gooden, the young pitching ace of the New York Mets. The seemingly inflated prices of $2 to $4 apiece will be a real value if Gooden fulfills predictions of long-term superstardom. Each card could be worth thousands of dollars one day.

Several years ago, however, there were similar predictions for Detroit Tiger pitcher Mark Fidrych. His baseball card rose quickly in value but came crashing down when his arm gave out. "You can speculate in baseball cards like penny stock, but pitchers are always the toughest investment," explained Robert Lemke, publisher of Baseball Card Magazine, published four times a year in Iola, Wis. "After all, you've got to realize that arm injuries can sink a career and card value along with it." Even Mickey Mantle's rookie baseball card has had its ups and down. It sold for $50 in the 1960s and was bid up to $2,500 in 1980, but dealers say recent sale prices have been considerably less.

Comic book speculators are also an active group. They snapped up last year's *Miracle Man* (issue No. 1) by Eclipse Comics because the press run was shorter than expected, and its value may increase. When DC Comics came out with a new *Superman* issue drawn by popular comic book artist John Byrne, collectors were poised to buy. After all, a May 1983 edition of *Amazing Spider-Man* (No. 252) is worth more than $3 simply because he wore a different costume. A classic Oct.- Nov. 1939 Marvel Comics (No. 1) featuring the Human Torch and Sub-Mariner could be worth as much as $20,000 if you can find the right collector. "As far as investing in comic books, the superhero types of the 1940s and 1950s hold up the best, with Superman, Batman, Captain America and Wonder Woman always very popular," said Robert Overstreet, publisher of the *Comic Book Price Guide*. "All the Marvel and DC comics produced in those characters' early days are highly sought after."

If you have something to sell, be a realist, because the vast majority of comic books and baseball cards really are worth little. The best bet for value in a comic book issue is if a character is introduced, undergoes a dramatic change or dies. A first issue can also be important. In baseball, the differences can be the success of the player, whether he competed in a major city that gave him high visibility and whether he has remained in the public eye. Sometimes an error can be made in information on the card; if it is corrected in subsequent printings, cards with the mistake can be valuable.

The condition the card or book is in when you try to sell it makes a big difference. Even a classic comic valued at hundreds of dollars is worth little if torn or wrinkled. True collectors keep their cards and books in plastic sleeves. If a comic book is too damaged, the value can come down 90 percent. Watch out for water damage and brittleness of pages. Books are graded as poor, good, fine, mint and pristine mint, with pristine condition perhaps doubling the value of a book that is in demand. Besides initial purchases in packs of gum, in sets and at newsstands, baseball cards are usually found in local trading stores that stock a large supply and are willing to buy from your collection.

Few people actively collect diamonds because of obvious price constraints and most experts chafe at their being considered an investment at all. Yet the idea frequently comes up whenever diamonds are purchased.

The sparkle of diamonds has become more brilliant lately, with many of the highest-quality stones appreciating 15 to 20 percent in value. However, while advertisements claim that "a diamond is forever," a quick look at the prices of these precious stones in the 1970s and 1980s indicates incredible volatility is a part of that longevity.

A one-carat flawless diamond, for example, cost $1,600 in 1972. It rose to $60,000 by 1979 because investors saw diamonds as an inflation hedge and the powerful DeBeers diamond cartel effectively boosted prices. Soon afterward, those inflated prices started their plummet, with that one-carat stone at $13,000 in 1985 and seemingly going nowhere. But it perked up again as DeBeers boosted prices again, made moves to tighten supply and began an advertising blitz. Demand increased among wealthy consumers, many of them from nations such as Japan, who realize that the highest-quality stones appreciate the most. As a result of all those machinations the same one-carat diamond is now worth more than $15,000, and many experts believe it may go higher.

Most diamond purchases are made in the spring or at Christmas. While diamonds can be sold relatively easily, it may be necessary to sell at wholesale price if you're in a hurry. Dealers buy at wholesale prices and sell at a marked-up retail price. It's important to find a reputable dealer you trust. Criteria for quality consists of the following: Cut (angles and proportions calculated to produce brilliance); carat weight (a carat equals 100 milligrams); clarity (the fewer flaws, the better); and color (with emphasis upon the "whitest" diamonds with the least color). The American Gem Society and the Gemological Institute of America both grade diamonds on quality and give certification to jewelers who pass a course in gemology. Obtain approval of the grade of your diamond from a gem laboratory that follows the standards of a reputable organization.

Buy diamonds in "true" light, rather than store lights, since stones sparkle more under flourescent lights. You should have your setting checked periodically to be sure the stone is properly in place. To insure your diamond, have it appraised, listing the color, cut and number of flaws. Always remember that diamonds are very speculative and that events such as political uncertainty or foreign currency changes can have a crazy effect on the market.

When it comes to true collecting, the value of quality art and antiques continues to set highs even though the inflation that sparked the initial boom in the 1970s hasn't made a comeback.

For example, a 31-inch bronze art deco sculpture by Paul Howard Manship, estimated by Butterfield's auction house to be worth $50,000, sold recently for a surprising $154,000. A Tiffany lamp valued at $50,000 five years ago sold for $137,500, with only two bidders willing to compete in such a lofty price arena. A Thomas Hart Benton "Jesse James" print that sold for $25 in the 1940s is now worth thousands of dollars. Selected individual works of New York artist Julian Schnabel, which a few years ago cost $3,000 apiece, were sold recently by the Sotheby Parke Bernet auction house for more than $50,000 each.

Be careful, however, even if your price range is closer to $100 than $1,000. Most collectibles as investments aren't anything you can really bank on. Prices tumbled during the recession. You can't sell them as easily as stocks, and their outlook is far harder to predict than interest rates. Making a real "killing" in art or antiques is an uncommon event. While Old Masters have ranked high in gains in investment value, many works of lesser quality or less well-known artists aren't worth any more now than they were several years ago. They have their ups and downs and are, as always, subject to the whims of the buying public. "No one should realistically buy art as an investment, but instead should buy primarily for enjoyment," counsels Warren P. Weitman Jr., senior vice president for Sotheby's. "If it appreciates, that's great, but aesthetic and emotional values should be the motivation." From an investment standpoint, it is important to buy the best you can afford. "The pieces whose prices will escalate tremendously are those of quality, not the more middle-of-the-road examples," said Jon King, who heads the American furniture and folk art department of San Francisco-based Butterfield's. "Remember that trends change. American furniture was popular in the 1920s, then interest died off, but it has been coming back in the last three years. Italian furniture isn't popular now, while French furniture is."

Here's a checklist of steps to follow when investing in art or antiques:

—Develop an eye for the items yourself, either by visiting museums, dealers or auction houses. You can easily get basic information free of charge.

—Take your time in shopping. Don't be pressured into making a quick decision. You'll have to live with your purchase. Some dealers will permit you to try the art or antique in your home on a test basis before buying.

—Look into the reputation of the dealer selling the art. Besides word-of-mouth recommendations, professional credentials can help. You can, for example, get a list of members of the Art Dealers Association of America, 575 Madison Ave., New York, N.Y. 10022.

—Dealers tend to be retailers, while auctions require homework but a chance to shop for the best deals. In the case of living artists, you can often contact them directly to make a purchase.

—To protect your investment, have it evaluated every three years by an appraiser who meets the qualifications of the Internal Revenue Service. You want the value placed on the item to hold up for tax reasons, whether you keep it, sell it or donate it to charity one day. It's also necessary for insurance purposes. Get the appraisal in writing.

—Get insurance through a rider to your homeowner's or renter's coverage. List each work and basic information about its history and condition. Keep a photo of each piece.

—Ask the dealer selling you the art or antique if he will help you sell it in the future.

—Realize that when you want to sell, sometimes the dealer will accept the item in trade for a more expensive piece of art or antique. But be careful, because he sometimes will give you only the value you paid for it, rather than a more current price.

—Maintain the piece of art or antique carefully, protecting it or polishing it as necessary to keep up its resale value. Only do refinishing work if you truly can do a professional job; damaging the work can reduce its value drastically.

—Buy what you can afford, and consider original prints or

graphics if paintings are too expensive. You'd be amazed at what you can buy for less than $100. Just make sure you like it and are realistic in your expectations for future price appreciation.

Millions of Americans collect limited-edition plates of silver, porcelain or other materials that can cost a few dollars or hundreds of dollars. Besides buying when these are first made available, sellers and buyers can also do business by telephone through the Bradford Exchange in Niles, Ill., which guarantees the transactions. The seller cost on transactions is high and, quite frankly, many items don't turn out to be worth much. There are also collector magazines that can help you in your quest to sell. Be wary of claims about rising value of such items and look carefully into whether they are as limited as advertised and whether there is a market for them later.

Many people do make money in collectibles. But always remember that just because you want to have an item doesn't mean someone else will want to buy it from you one day.

6   Saver's Choice

"They took away my IRA."

That's the battle cry of many Americans these days. Had tax reformers done less in the way of changing tax brackets but simply kept the individual retirement account deduction intact for all workers, they might be considered heroes right now.

Americans, you see, got downright proud of their IRAs. I've heard from hundreds of readers the last few years from all income levels who were either seeking advice about their IRAs or bragging about how shrewd they'd been with their IRAs. Those accounts became as American as apple pie, turning saving into an organized pastime. The beauty of the IRA was that it was so simple. Financial institutions were battling for your business in earnest, with the blessing of Uncle Sam to boot.

Not that a few folks didn't get a little mixed up even in the old days. Once a fellow worker of mine and several colleagues were talking over financial matters when he mentioned how he'd been getting his financial house in order. "Those IRAs are great," he said enthusiastically. "I think so much of them that I've opened one for each of my children." He was immediately pummeled by his chums, who shouted that he was a "dope" for mistakenly opening those accounts for his preteen brood.

Because of compromise and the fact that it offered a quick-fix of additional revenues to a nation saddled with a massive federal deficit, the IRA isn't so simple anymore. It's damaged as a marketable product because of its new complexity, which folks won't take the time to figure out, and because it won't apply equally to everyone. "After the same number of IRA investments as usual for the 1986 tax year, we feel they may pretty much peter out," predicted one executive of a big New York bank.

IRAs have never turned out to be as big money makers as financial institutions had hoped. Investors were fickle, willing to move accounts for a better interest rate or bonus or promise of big stock gains. But they did bring in plenty of money that institutions hope to retain. "From now on we're going to emphasize that IRA is attractive because of the tax deferral," said a member of the top brass of a major brokerage house.

The IRA, of course, isn't dead. You can still make money with it, considerably more than if the investment money was in a taxable investment. Workers not covered by a retirement plan can still deduct up to $2,000 a year in IRA contributions from income on federal returns ($2,250 for one-income couples). A worker with a company pension and up to $25,000 in adjusted gross income, or $40,000 for a couple, can continue deducting $2,000 a year. Then things get complicated. Americans making $25,000 to $35,000 or couples making $40,000 to $50,000 receive a lesser deduction. But those at the end of that range will be allowed a minimum deduction of $200 even if the formula would provide less.

Taxpayers with incomes above $50,000 on a joint return and $35,000 on single returns will not be entitled to a deduction, and for married couples it won't be possible to get around that even by filing separate returns. They can, however, continue contributing and receive a tax deferral nonetheless.

One mutual fund company sent out more than 1 million mailings to customers about the fact that tax-deferred compounding is still "a good thing." Assume a $2,000 annual contribution over a 25-year period, with a 28 percent tax bracket and a healthy 10 percent investment return, it pointed out. A tax-deferred IRA with no deduction would eventually total $216,364, while an investment without tax deferral paying the same return would reach only $155,782. Both deductible and nondeductible IRAs will outperform regular savings accounts in the long run. However, the old belief that you were still ahead putting money in an IRA even if you pulled your money out after six years and paid the penalties isn't quite the same. In the case of the nondeductible IRA, that time period has now been stretched to about 12 years.

Under the new law, stock investments in IRAs may become more popular because the preferential capital gains treatment is eliminated and all stock market profits will be taxed at regular rates; the IRA will provide one place where taxes on those profits can be deferred for years.

So while the IRA isn't what it used to be, it is well worth considering. It remains important that you put your contribution in early in the tax year so that your money is sheltered sooner. There is no denying, however, that many people will opt instead for competing products such as tax-exempt municipal bonds, single-premium whole life insurance, tax-deferred annuities and company 401(k) plans. That's one reason why many banks are already offering products such as annuities.

Saving is always a good deal, and a regular program of putting money away each month has been the best way for generations of Americans to accumulate wealth. Most of that saving has been done through bank accounts. Because of the new tax laws, bank accounts get a bit of a boost. Lower tax brackets mean many savers will get to keep more of what they save, making fixed-rate investments look better to them. Not changing, however, are the stiff penalties for early withdrawal of money kept in certificates of deposit. And, of course, interest rates have to be attractive before savers are willing to tie up their money.

I used to hear from one telephone caller every six months or so. In a crackly old voice, he'd always ask what I'd heard lately from economists about interest rates. I considered this sort of a once-in-a-while service for someone who didn't have the wherewithal to seek conventional financial help.

After several years of this, however, I grew curious. Following some gentle questioning, my anonymous caller opened up a bit and admitted that he had three jumbo CDs rolling over at his bank. That, my friends, is a cool $300,000! No wonder he was so concerned!

Americans have generally had a strained relationship with their bankers, one made worse by this era of increasing fees for services.

"I no longer trust the veracity of banks because not only are we nickeled-and-dimed to death with petty service charges, but they never offer information," one irate reader stated in a letter. "I am tired of questioning the origin of some of the postings on my monthly checking statement and consider compound interest figures a maze."

A cartoon that sums up the situation in the minds of many people is the one that shows an anxious man sitting hat-in-hand in a bank executive's office. The banker gives his guest a long look and says: "While it may be true, Mr. Pedigrew, that we have made some unfortunate loans to foreign countries, we do not make unfortunate loans to individuals."

These days, the nation's banks aren't nearly as unhappy as you are about low savings interest rates. Such rates, after all, help their bottom line considerably because they're paying out little in interest while receiving high returns from consumer loans and credit cards.

Socked hardest is the elderly American on a fixed income, who may have to dig into investment principal. The mix of investments has changed, with fewer people willing to commit long-term for rates only modestly higher than those of more liquid accounts. Most banks have tried to keep their passbook rate at 5.5 percent rather than making a cut. The real motive behind that is that a changed passbook rate would likely become a variable rate, rather than fixed. A variable rate would have to go up when other rates rise, perhaps resulting in a lofty passbook rate one day.

"The question we keep getting is, 'Don't you have anything that pays better than this?' " said a senior vice president at one of the nation's biggest banks. "While I could suggest putting some money into CDs of 10 years or more to get more interest, I really think most people don't want to go long-term." His bank is seeing more money go into the tax-exempt money market fund it offers through a mutual fund group. Another bank has come up with a popular new account that offers a rate that's fixed quarterly and pays more than a money market account.

"The new tax laws are unlikely to help either the amount Americans save or the rates being paid," said one bank economist. "We're supposed to be moving from a consuming economy to an investing economy, but a question mark remains after the investing part."

It's still important to get the best rate you can. Shop at least three financial institutions, then consider convenience and confidence in the institution before choosing. Consolidate money in one place if it means fewer fees. Always have in mind what services you personally use the most, so that you'll be able to compute exactly what you'll wind up paying in terms of fees on a regular basis. Pay only for services you need, and don't opt for the so-called "streamlined" package if it's expensive or confining.

It is possible to receive higher interest on your account if you place your money with a bank or savings and loan in another city or state. You should, however, compute whether the move is really worth the effort to you. According to the *100 Highest Yields* newsletter, the nation's highest money market account rate in late 1986 was Colonial National Bank, Wilmington, Del., at a 7.25 percent effective annual yield. The top one-year rate was Alamo Savings, San Antonio, at 7.71 percent, and the best five-year certificate was Empire of America Savings, San Francisco, with an 8.46 percent effective annual yield. All were considerably higher than the average yields being paid around the country at that time. Remember that such rankings change weekly and that lists of top-yielding institutions as ranked by *100 Highest Yields* are carried in newspapers around the country. (In addition, weekly issues are available for an $84 annual subscription from 100 Highest Yields, 860 Federal Hwy. One, North Palm Beach, Fla. 33408-3825.)

Some institutions seeking out-of-state business have toll-free telephone numbers. Whether they do or not, it is vital to talk only with a knowledgeable bank officer; tell how much you wish to invest and for how long; receive a pre-assigned account number; get the specific address and branch of the institution, and obtain the bank's identification number. If you use the mail, there's a time delay of three or four days and the rate in effect depends on when they receive the money. If you decide to wire the money from your current bank, make the money payable to the new institution rather than any officer. Wire it to the exact address. The wire charge may cost $5 to $10, that charge being arbitrary from institution to institution.

Always make sure that your money is in an institution in which deposits are insured to $100,000 by the Federal Deposit Insurance Corp. Savings and loan deposits are similarly insured by the Federal Savings & Loan Insurance Corp. This is important, since some state and privately-insured institutions have had financial problems in recent years.

You don't have to stick with a bank or savings and loan to save effectively, however. Amid the financial revolution of the deregulated 1980s, it's particularly easy to overlook the credit union. It's ever so common and hardly on the cutting edge of high finance. Yet this basic operation is changing with the times, weathering most anything the modern era throws at it.

A well-run credit union is a good place to put some of your money. It often offers superior deals, among them fewer fees for services such as checks (called share drafts) and lower credit charges. There are nearly 18,000 credit unions, most organized around employers, but many tied to religious, community or school groups, according to the Credit Union National Association. That's down several hundred in recent years, the result of mergers and liquidations for economic reasons such as plant closings and layoffs.

Remarkably, their savings deposits have jumped by one-fourth, to $125 billion. Dollars are growing, thanks to the continuing emphasis on savings that began with payroll deductions. Most of these non-profit organizations offer competitive rates and a full range of financial products, with small or no fees. Some have automated teller machines. Loan volume has been down, however, because of the pinch of special financing offered by car manufacturers. Car loans remain the bread and butter of credit unions, along with small personal loans. At some larger credit unions, mortgages, usually with low origination fees, are also available. More and more credit unions are offering credit cards, with an average interest of about 14 percent, far better than most banks. A third of them require no annual fees.

"We offer a toll-free telephone number 24 hours a day, so you can get your balance, see if money has been transferred and find out if checks have cleared, all without coming to the office," explained an executive with Corporate America Federal Credit Union, Elmhurst, Ill., which has 13 branches nationwide and represents 30,000 employees of 35 companies. That group's most popular programs include a purchase deal on used Hertz rental cars and a Visa card with a low interest rate, no annual fee and a 25-day grace period. Its car loans are also competitive.

"Our safe deposit box rentals are popular," said another credit union official. "We also feature 'instant loans,' in which the decision is made within one hour. Essentially, we've achieved full-service banking activities." Like many credit unions, all that's required to remain a member is to keep $5 in a share account. While one must have been an employee of a participating company at some point, spouses, parents, siblings and children are permitted to join.

"With us, it's once a member, always a member," said a spokesman for the 21,000-member Hamilton Standard Federal Credit Union, Windsor Locks, Conn. "Our most-used services aren't all that fancy, such as direct deposit of paychecks and a payroll deduction for our Christmas club."

There are more than 10,000 federally insured credit unions. Nearly 5,000 state-chartered credit unions are also federally insured, according to the National Credit Union Administration, a federal body that insures accounts to $100,000. The remaining credit unions are privately insured. Though problems privately-insured savings and loans have encountered don't relate to credit unions, there has been a strong movement to convert from private to federal insurance. In addition, the number of problem credit unions has been declining steadily. The National Credit Union Administration conducts annual examinations and semiannual reviews of financial statements. If merger is required, business goes on as usual. In liquidations, payouts are made to members from a pooled insurance fund to which all credit unions have contributed 1 percent of their shares.

Work frequently is the tie-in to saving on a regular basis for many Americans. Though the IRA has been the "big daddy" of retirement plans, it is important for self-employed workers to keep in mind that they may still set up, in addition to an IRA, a Keogh plan in which they may take an annual deduction of up to $30,000. In the case of a profit-sharing plan, the deduction is limited to the lesser of $30,000 or 13 percent of net self-employment income. For a money-purchase pension plan, the limitation is the lesser of $30,000 or 20 percent of net self-employment income. A defined-benefit plan may provide a deduction as high as 100 percent of net self-employment income. Since tax law changes haven't blunted its features and because there are fewer shelters around now, a Keogh makes sense if you qualify.

By changing IRA eligibility, the new tax laws make a lot of corporate programs look good. However, many of the shrewdest shoppers for investments overlook even better opportunities offered where they work. Some of the best company savings plans, in which the employer also kicks in a substantial part, are ignored by workers. As with many benefits, employees are either confused or they tend to shrug off the basic concept of benefits for all except emergency situations.

"Our surveys have found the typical savings plan allows a worker to contribute one to six percent of pay, and the company will match a portion of what the worker put in, often 50 cents on the dollar and in some cases dollar-for-dollar," explained an executive with a benefits consultant firm. "I think few of us are savvy enough to do better than that with our money elsewhere."

Among companies offering such plans, the investment is often its own stock, though there's a trend toward additional choices such as money market funds, stock funds and fixed-interest investments. Such matching thrift plans, generally offered in addition to regular pension or profit-sharing plans, are hard to beat.

Don't forget that the maximum deferred amount in a company 401(k) income plan starting with the 1987 tax year is $7,000 annually, down from $30,000 in prior years. In addition, neither an employer's matching contributions to a 401(k) plan nor the income on those contributions and the employee's selective contributions is eligible for hardship withdrawals.

Investment plans are just the tip of an iceberg of employee benefits of which workers often don't take advantage. A lot of employees don't really become interested in a variety of benefits, particularly retirement benefits, until they're 45 years old. They don't know what they have when they're hired and never bother to find out later. In the 1980s, growth of employee benefits came to a halt and the trend is toward controlling costs. Benefits such as dental care have become common and there is very slow movement toward more "cafeteria-style" plans in which workers choose benefits they desire most. There's modest growth in child care. "When you're looking for a job, you should ask basic questions of employ-

ees, particularly what the pension plan would provide at age
65 with 30 years of service," advised one benefits consultant.
"Be sure to ask what multiple of your salary would be received
in life insurance, also whether there is a disability program,
and what portion you'll have to pay for medical costs."

Always obtain information on pension and profit-sharing,
something legally required of employers. Keep in mind that
smaller companies often don't offer as wide a range of benefits.

Some other considerations on employee benefits:

—Find out what the maximum limit is on what you personally must pay in medical costs and the cost for basic sur-
gical operations. If, for example, you're considering having a
child, it's worthwhile to know exactly how much you'll pay.

—Make sure beneficiaries listed on your company life insurance are up-to-date, particularly following a divorce or
death. There have been many incidents of "surprise" recipi-
ents.

—Go over double health coverage when both spouses work,
to see which policy is best used for certain types of coverage.
See whose coverage covers what.

—Check out the vesting schedule in your firm's pension or
profit-sharing plan before you leave a company to take another job.

—Realize that medical benefits usually stop the day you
leave your job, so you'll probably need supplemental benefits
if there's a delay before your next job.

7　Homes and Home Equity Loans

In the classic Frank Capra film *It's a Wonderful Life*, leading man James Stewart was a hero because he succeeded in helping average folks attain the American dream: a home of their own. He battled valiantly against those in high places who might try to take away that dream.

Compare that to a telephone call I received recently from a reader who didn't want any part of that dream. "Everybody these days is calling a home an investment and that's bunk," he complained. "It's not an investment at all. I ask you, how many times have you ever had to paint a stock certificate or fix the furnace of a mutual fund?"

While there may be something to that opinion, if ever proof was needed that owning a home is still considered the American dream, the new tax laws are it. Reformers in Congress made certain that "home sweet home" will remain the best tax shelter for Americans simply by keeping the interest on it tax-deductible. But they also fiddled around enough with the various aspects of homeowning to make formulating a sensible tax strategy quite a challenge. That's because the new lower individual brackets slice the value of that deduction for many Americans.

Perhaps the most dramatic effect of the new tax laws involves the home equity loan, already on a roll and now suddenly the hottest financial product going. Let's examine it before moving on to some of the more basic financial considerations of home ownership in the 1980s.

The national advertising blitz and all-out rate wars in some cities indicate just how much the nation's banks, brokerage firms and finance companies think they can profit from the modern home equity loan. With deductibility of interest on traditional consumer loans being gradually phased out over five years, this loan, which permits you to tap the equity built up in your home, remains fully deductible. Just don't forget that taking out such a loan also increases the potential that you might lose your beloved home one day if you're not careful.

Under the new tax laws, the deduction on a home equity loan is limited to loans that are no greater than the initial cost of your residence or second home, plus any improvements you've made to it. For example, someone who bought a home for $100,000 and added $15,000 in improvements could deduct interest on a loan of up to $115,000. There's one option in the law that lets homeowners borrow more than the original purchase price plus improvements and still deduct interest, so long as the money is used to pay for education or medical expenses. Don't forget to keep receipts or canceled checks that indicate the specific use of the money, should the IRS raise questions later.

While a home equity loan is more or less a second mortgage, it differs in that it is not a lump-sum payment but a revolving line of credit in which money is taken out as needed by check or credit card. In most cases, lenders offer a credit line of 75 to 80 percent of a home's fair market value. Different home equity loans have different repayment requirements. Some firms, such as Merrill Lynch & Co., permit customers to pay only the interest due, with principal due at the end of 10 years (and even then the loan is renewable). Other institutions have more stringent payback requirements. In all cases, it is easy to see how a borrower could wind up letting things slide, losing track of how much is owed and getting into serious debt problems. With your home as collateral, the lending institution has little to lose while, on the other hand, you could lose your home. Or one day heirs might inherit a home which, it turns out, is more debt than substance.

The loan charge on a home equity loan has typically been a variable rate of one to three percentage points higher than the prime lending rate (which, for example, was 7.5 percent in late 1986), though increased competition is changing that. Rate wars have cropped up in various parts of the country with "come-ons" of less than six percent, and further competition could cut them even more. When shopping—and the variety of rates makes it very important to shop around—always check out how long the introductory rate will stay in force and what rate index will be used after that point. Many lenders also charge "points," which are up-front fees representing two to three percent of the total loan amount. There may also be closing costs of up to $400, but in areas where there is greater competition these are being waived.

Lenders see the home equity loan as a golden opportunity, most all of them eagerly pointing out that $3 trillion in homeowner equity is available. "Overall, the cost of consumer credit will increase sharply under tax reform," said Chuck Humm, vice president in the credit management group of Merrill Lynch, who oversees its home equity program and considers it the most reasonably-priced choice. "And people who say the consumer doesn't care about the cost of credit are dead wrong." Spokesmen for New York's Chemical Bank point out that they've beefed up their home equity loan staffing considerably to coincide with the new tax laws, while First National Bank of Chicago estimates that one-fourth of all its mortgage borrowing these days is being done by customers who wish to consolidate their debt.

All is not equal under home equity loans. Because the loan amount is based on the initial purchase price of the home, someone who bought his home years ago when prices were low probably won't have as much borrowing power as his neighbor who bought his home last year. For that reason, financial planners tell me, some Americans are actually looking at selling their present homes and buying similar ones simply to gain more borrowing power through a home equity loan. That's quite an extreme move that had better be proved by the figures before any action is taken.

In fact, because of all the costs tacked on to home equity loans, it's a good idea to add up every one of these fees so that you can see if you're really getting as good a deal as it appears. Carefully compare the cost of the home equity loan to refinancing of your mortgage or taking out a second mortgage. Many home equity loans have no ceiling as to how high the rate charged can go, so you might conceivably wind up paying some truly onerous rates if economic conditions change. That could affect your ability to pay as well, and falling behind in payments on a home equity loan could mean loss of your home just as easily as falling behind in the payments on your conventional mortage. So decide if that risk is worth it. Don't act capriciously, or sign up simply because it is being touted as the "in" thing to do under the new tax laws.

I've run into a few people who have bragged about their home equity loans as status symbols, not unlike a premium charge card. I don't think that is really the logical extension of the philosophy Frank Capra was pushing in *It's a Wonderful Life*.

Going beyond the home equity loan, other aspects of home-owning under the new tax laws aren't like the good old days, either. For example, how good a deal owning a home really is depends in part upon your individual tax bracket. The after-tax cost of owning a home will increase for high-income taxpayers in 1987 because the value of their deduction will be diminished by the lower marginal tax brackets. Out-of-pocket expenses will increase. For that same reason, a vacation home is likely to look less attractive to many Americans these days. "Someone who was in a 50 percent tax bracket getting $4,200 in deductions on his home each year will, in a 35 percent bracket, see those deductions slide to $2,940, so you can't say that won't be noticed," said one real estate agent.

Some experts are convinced that this may result in a decline in prices of more expensive homes over the next several years. Others also believe that the overall tax burden will gradually increase for homeowners despite the federal tax cuts. "I think the homeowner can expect increases in property taxes as the federal government continues to pursue its policy of placing more of the tax burden on states," predicted Ronald Poe, president of the Mortgage Bankers Association of America. Of course, plenty of traditional special treatment remains for the home, such as the fact that the government still won't tax profits from the sale of a home so long as the proceeds are used to buy another home. And, like always, folks 55 years of age and older who sell a home without reinvesting the proceeds will still be able to avoid taxes on the first $125,000 of profit.

The main reason why homes are being touted as big winners under the new tax laws is simply that most other shelters have vanished. In reality, the biggest boost to the housing industry over the next few years will likely come from interest rates remaining low, rather than anything that happened in Washington.

Yet everyone must set an individual debt strategy. "Because mortgage interest is deductible and other kinds of interest are not, I believe the best strategy is for the homebuyer to get as large a mortgage as possible on his home," advised Kent Colton, executive vice president of the National Association of Home Builders. The trend to 15-year mortgages, which now represent nearly 20 percent of new loans, should accelerate. "The 15-year mortgage, though generally more attractive at higher interest rates, is probably a good idea with or without the new tax laws," said James W. Christian, chief economist for the U.S. League of Savings Institutions. "Buyers are realizing that, during the first five years of a 15-year mortgage, you build up seven times as much equity as you would with a 30-year mortgage." (Of course, most 30-year mortgages give the homeowner the option of putting in extra dollars each month, or an extra payment each year, in order to pay off principal more quickly. In addition, bi-weekly mortgages speed up the payment procedure and have a similar cost-cutting effect over the life of the loan.)

More renters may decide to buy a home simply because it is one of the few shelters left and because of potential hikes in rent as landlords who have lost tax breaks try to make up their costs. Less incentive for developers to build multi-unit buildings or rehabilitate older buildings may also create scarcity and add to rents. But all of these worries should be tempered by the current high apartment vacancies in many parts of the nation. It's also worth keeping in mind that, aside from lack of money for a downpayment for a home, many people rent to have greater flexibility in their lifestyle and to have fewer upkeep and financial responsibilities.

If you don't yet own a home, carefully weigh how much better off you might be in buying rather than renting before you decide whether it's worth it. According to a study by Century 21 Real Estate Corp. of eight of the nation's largest cities, annual savings for an individual in a 38.5 percent tax bracket in 1987 by buying rather than renting ranges from $100 in Atlanta to $6,000 in Chicago. Only in New York City, with its escalating house prices, is it actually less expensive to rent than to buy.

However, the study predicted that as more buyers realize how much the new tax law reduces the after-tax value of home write-offs—and it does significantly—prices may fall in many parts of the country.

The type of folks who buy homes has also changed. A great many single people are homeowners these days, so it's not just the domain of a traditional family with two children and a dog. Your prime consideration should be your ability to handle the financial aspects of homeowning over the long haul. A home can, for example, be a major millstone around a family's neck to a degree that it can cause significant emotional problems that can pull the family apart.

Once you've decided what you can afford and what your salary expectations are in meeting your responsibilities, set your criteria for a home. Know what you want in terms of location (there, I've said it, all of you real estate brokers out there!) and proximity to good schools, churches and parks. Check our municipal services such as sewers, street lights and police protection. Transportation, shopping and cultural and recreational activities might also be on your checklist. The same things that make a home attractive when you buy it will also make it attractive when you wish to sell it to someone one day.

A conventional single-family home is still likely to sell better than a condominium, though in some cities condos are very attractive. Touted as a home that offers an easier lifestyle, the actual purchase of a condo will nonetheless require the same amount of effort as buying a conventional home. In addition, purchasing a condo includes buying community property, and charges for its care are assessed through a monthly fee that is added to your mortgage costs. Condominiums have been popular with retirees and young professionals who want the benefits of home ownership without the worries of maintenance. Young married couples also find a more modest condominium to be an excellent way to establish credit and build equity.

The dream of home ownership is already a reality for millions. Six out of 10 American families own their own homes, and with the blessing of the new tax laws those numbers are expected to increase. For first-timers hoping to join that home-owning group, there are important steps to consider, such as finding the money for a down payment.

Some lucky folks can take advantage of an offer from parents or other relatives for a downpayment, often with no financial strings attached. Most other people are not so lucky. They must seek other methods of raising that initial capital.

Remember that most institutions would like you to place 10 to 20 percent down, and that the median price of an existing single-family these days is around $80,000. A regular weekly or monthly savings program is a good way to get started toward that goal. While that's the best game plan, the positive tax aspects of owning a home might even make it financially worthwhile to take money out of an existing IRA, company pension plan, insurance policy or Keogh plan for a downpayment—even though there are penalties involved.

It pays to have been in uniform. If you've been in the armed forces, you may be able to get a loan for 100 percent of the cost of the home through a mortgage backed by the Veterans Administration. Application is made through a conventional lender. The Federal Housing Administration can cover up to 95 percent of the cost of a home mortgage, though there'll be a ceiling on the mortgage amount. In addition, some lending institutions also will write mortgages for 95 percent of the costs if you qualify, although this usually means that closing costs will be higher.

All mortgages and terms are not alike. Hand-in-hand with securing the downpayment is choosing the type of mortgage. Basically two types of mortgages are available for the home-buyer: fixed and adjustable-rate. Before you meet formally with the lender, do some shopping to find out just what is offered in your community. Pick up brochures and keep a file on basic information. A fixed-rate mortgage means the rate is constant. If you're the type of person who lives on a budget and needs to know how much your monthly payment will be, it's the choice for you. There are 15- and 30-year terms. The 15-year loan has been gaining popularity with homebuyers who realize that it puts more of their initial payments into equity rather than interest expenses. For a modestly higher payment, they'll be able to pay off their loan in half the time.

Adjustable-rate mortgages (ARM's) fluctuate depending on the index to which the loan is tied. They generally offer lower initial interest rates than conventional fixed-rate loans. ARM's can rise or fall every six to 12 months, depending on the underlying index, whether tied to Treasury securities or to a computation such as the Federal Home Loan Bank Board's median cost of funds. Consider a variable loan only if you know your budget can withstand fluctuations. Don't forget that the rate can go down as well, and in that case you obviously benefit. The balloon mortgage, another option, is a loan that requires smaller monthly payments. But, at the end of the term agreed upon (usually 5 years), the balance must be paid off. Balloons can be a big financial headache if all does not come together properly at the end of that period. Balloons were responsible for many foreclosures during the hey-day of rapidly-rising home prices.

Whichever mortgage you choose, your homebuying decision should be based upon your own financial character and comfort level with debt. If you can't enjoy the simple pleasures of life because all of your money is going into your home, or you'll be losing sleep over whether your mortgage will be adjusted upward next year, rethink your strategy.

Although Will Rogers exhorted Americans to buy land because they aren't making any more of it, there are no assurances these days that your home's value will increase sufficiently to make it worth taking on a truly heavy debt load.

That load may be even greater than you imagine. Many costs associated with purchasing a home often go overlooked. That's in addition to purchases such as a lawnmower and decorating (although even those items are often an expensive surprise for first-time buyers). Many other costs, which can add 5 to 6 percent to the overall price of the home, should be considered before you sign any papers.

At the time of the loan application, for example, lenders require that you pay an application fee that can run from $50 to as much as $300. A title search, which makes sure no legal problems are involved in ownership of the home, can sometimes run as high as $1,500.

An attorney well-versed in real estate transactions should

represent you at the closing and also answer questions to help avoid problems later, all at a cost that can average around $700. Mortgage insurance isn't always required, depending on your state and how big a downpayment you've made, but you might have to take out a term policy equal to one percent of home price. You may have to settle with the previous owner for partially-paid real estate taxes or other costs, such as heating oil left in the tank. Homeowner insurance is required by almost all institutions and must be brought to the closing. The annual premium is usually more than $300. Factors such as whether the home has smoke detectors or deadbolt locks on the doors may affect the size of that premium. Property taxes depend on the state and county governments.

A "point," once again, is the upfront charge assessed by the financial institution and is equal to one percent of the mortgage. Depending on the institution, there can be as many as four points involved in the transaction.

Once you've taken the big step, paid the movers and are an honest-to-goodness homeowner, remember that how you treat that home will have the greatest bearing on its value should you wish to sell it at some future date.

When I was a youngster, my father, a home remodeling buff, would take the family out on Sunday afternoons to look at homes. Sometimes they were new homes from which he'd get ideas for remodeling; sometimes they were homes that might be suitable for remodeling. "This home will always be worth something, it's built like a rock," he'd say as he did his once-over. Or: "The guy who tried to fix this place up did a 'shoemaker job' that makes it worth less, not more." He told us how important it was to have a nice kitchen and bathroom when selling, how you shouldn't put more money into a home than the neighborhood merited and that a fresh coat of paint can add thousands of dollars to an asking price. While at a tender age I was bored to tears by such homilies, I must admit that I keep hearing those same things come back to me whenever I report on the home market. Such information is passed down from generation to generation because, in the scheme of things, a home has always been considered one of the venerated aspects of life.

Home remodeling is a booming business, with the average family spending nearly $1,000 a year. Remodeling is done for a number of reasons, such as enlarging or adding a room to meet the family's needs and, hopefully, adding to the value of the home. Before you go overboard, keep in mind that a few cans of paint can often do the trick. Most new homeowners will fix the property to their liking anyway when they move in, and they might not even like your ambitious decorating schemes anyway.

A few years back, a real estate agent gave me a tour of a rather mundane-looking ranch-style home that turned out to be very different once inside. While the family appeared to be as regular as any suburban family, there were hot pink curtains in every room and enough mirrors to daze even Narcissus. But the *piece de resistance* was the basement, which the owner referred to as "our lower living level." Besides featuring an enormous dark leather wet bar, the basement was filled with large black custom wrought-iron rails twisted in a variety of swirling round shapes and riveted to the walls as room dividers and "accent pieces." "Can you believe we've got $25,000 worth of wrought iron down here?" the owner asked the prospective buyer as he leaned on one of the monstrosities shaped like a distorted wagon wheel.

I envisioned the next owner of that home—who would certainly not be me—using crowbars to rip out that enormous financial outlay. To say the least, the owner's creativity detracted from his home's selling price.

Keep in mind the value of your property in relationship to your neighborhood so that any remodeling work is in line with that pricing scheme. Don't try to make your home the most expensive in your neighborhood, for it'll make it tougher to sell. Seek professional advice if you intend to undertake a truly substantial project, and don't turn work over to any construction company without thoroughly checking out its reputation and getting everything in writing. Also keep in mind that it is much more expensive to add a room to a home than you probably think, so buying a bigger home in the first place might be a better long-term answer.

When it comes time to sell your home, you can use a real estate broker or sell it yourself. Neither way is right, but whichever means is chosen, your home will likely sell more quickly if you've done a thorough clean-up and made paint touch-ups as necessary. Some sellers go so far as to place some of their wardrobe in storage in order to make closets appear larger, or to remove furniture to give the home a more airy look.

Not every real estate broker is everyone's cup of tea. When it comes time to sell your home and you want a broker to help you with it, do your homework in selecting the right one. Get recommendations from friends or interview a handful of agents to see who knows your area the best. Make sure they can show the home during the hours when most people are looking. Feel confident that he or she is the type of person you want representing you and that an honest attempt will be made to get a price for your home which is comparable to other homes in your neighborhood.

The seller has plenty of choices when it comes to offering the home, though the goal, of course, is to sell for a fair price. Once you have selected a broker, you will have to decide how you want to list the property.

The most-common "exclusive right to sell" gives the agent sole possession of your listing for a period of time, usually three months. It will be placed on a multiple listing service so that all other agents can see that it is available. The broker will get the commission for selling the home, although the commission is split in half if another broker finds the prospective buyer. (Another modified form is the "exclusive agency listing" in which the broker with whom you've listed is the only one who can get a commission, although you are free yourself to sell it and avoid the commission.) Finally, the "open listing" gives the broker you signed with the right to sell your home, but permits other brokers to show and sell it.

In addition, you can also sell it yourself and not pay any commission.

Remember that the listing contract is a legal document, so look it over and be certain that you agree to all terms before you sign. Agents typically charge five to six percent of the selling price, though this can be open to negotiation.

While it's true that real estate brokers offer helpful information, give your home exposure and screen prospective buyers, they exact that substantial fee for their efforts. So there understandably is an increase in the number of "For Sale By Owner" signs on lawns these days, as more people go about the job of hawking their homes themselves. Selling by owner works best, of course, when the market is strong and buyers are beating down the door. In most markets, however, selling a home without professional assistance requires a lot of time and effort.

Some people selling their own home overprice it and are offended if anyone looking at it says anything negative. "All they could say was that the front room was crooked, when my Frank worked an entire winter making that floor as straight as could be," one seller told me of an argument she had with potential buyers. "When she kept saying how dinky the bedrooms were, I was about to throw her out!" Not the best way to make a sale.

To figure out a fair price, read classified advertisements and check out prices of comparable homes in your neighborhood. Some brokers might even give you a price for free without obligation. Be sure to point out your home's best features in your newspaper advertisement. You must be willing to hang around your home at set times or during open-house days to show it, something most sellers find annoying (particularly when the prospective buyer doesn't show up as promised). Have a blank contract handy should someone make a serious bid and have a lawyer who can review the contract. Make sure the prospective buyer is qualified. Ask for a recent pay stub, then get a deposit of at least $1,000 or more at the time both parties sign the contract. You should be prepared to help explain available financing in the area if your purchaser is a first-time buyer.

If you're content with your present home, but not with your mortgage, you can join the ranks of homeowners who have refinanced their mortgage. Refinancing took off when interest rates dropped and lower monthly payments looked like a good deal. Refinancing is not unlike a first-time purchase, and you should follow the basic steps that you took in applying for your original mortgage. Shop around, going to your current lender first to see what sort of deal he'll come up with to keep your business.

Because of renegotiation fees that include points and application fees, you can expect to spend several thousand dollars. So, to make refinancing worthwhile, the new mortgage rate should be at least two percentage points lower than what you're now paying and you should be intending to stay in the home for at least three years.

Still another aspect of the American homeowning dream involves rental property. A lot of average folks made money by saving up to buy small apartment buildings, but that part of the dream has lost its magic.

Under the new tax laws, mortgage interest and property taxes are deductible only on first and second homes. A special rule applies to treatment of a vacation home used as a residence when its rental use is minimal, meaning less than 15 days during the year. In that case, the gross rental income is not reportable for tax purposes. However, expenses attributable to the property are not deductible, except for interest, property taxes and casualty losses. In addition, landlords with adjusted gross income of more than $150,000 will no longer be able to write off more expenses than the amount of rental income generated. That could very well mean the difference between making and losing money on the proposition for many landlords.

Investors who actively manage a property and handle major responsibilities such as selection of tenants and setting of rents do have certain advantages under the new laws. Those with adjusted gross incomes of less than $100,000 can use up to

$25,000 in tax losses to offset other income. That shrinks as income exceeds $100,000 and no longer exists once income reaches $150,000.

Ah, home sweet home. Like many other aspects of the new tax laws, it isn't such a simple structure anymore.

8   New Life for Insurance

The insurance industry is receiving a real shot in the arm from the new tax laws. Rather than solely provide insurance, many new products are honest-to-goodness investments with advantages over competing instruments now hobbled by tax restrictions.

Not only insurance companies, but banks and brokerage firms are touting the likes of single-premium whole life insurance and tax-deferred annuities. So long as you watch out for fees and sometimes overstated yields, these choices can provide some diversity to your overall strategy to make money under the new tax laws.

"Things have changed," said Joseph W. Jordan, insurance-product manager with PaineWebber Inc. as he leaned back in a conference-room chair to pop in a video cassette that featured baseball great Tom Seaver making a pitch for a deferred annuity that divides its portfolio among stocks and bonds. "Top management is actually treating me as well as the mutual fund people."

Takes some getting used to, this new visibility. You see, the average American has never been too keen on talking about topics such as life insurance, making a will or health coverage, to name a few. They conjure up too many images of our human vulnerability. And the relationship many people have had with the insurance industry hasn't always been a love affair, either.

A few years ago, I interviewed an insurance agent on a television talk show and asked him about the problems some folks have dealing with pushy insurance sales people. The fellow, a thoughtful sort who was also an instructor in financial planning, told me in no uncertain terms: "If someone insists on trying to sell you coverage you don't want, throw him right out of your living room!"

Seemed fair enough. But the next day, I heard from another insurance agent who screamed that my interviewee was an idiot, a downright dolt. When asked why, the angry agent responded: "Because anyone in insurance with half a mind knows that you sell insurance in the kitchen, not the living room!"

As anyone who's ever been asked by an insurance salesperson if they've "got a minute" can attest, insurance and annuities are difficult propositions that don't seem to be getting any easier to grasp. However, these days not only are some policies receiving a decent return, but their tax deferral features offer some advantages that weren't affected by the new tax laws.

For example, the $7.6 million package that the Tampa Bay Buccaneers reportedly offered star running back Bo Jackson to try to convince him to forsake baseball for pro football was loaded with hundreds of thousands of dollars in annuities.

In the late 1970s, I was a guest speaker at a national conference on life insurance that was considering the need to modernize policies to cope with the high interest rates and inflation of that period. A young man who identified himself as an actuary raised his hand and declared: "Let's face it. The only reason our companies sell any whole life insurance at all is because some salesmen could sell anything!" He was overstating his case out of frustration. But the industry wheels already were in motion to tie traditional insurance with more modern instruments so it could do battle with higher-yield alternatives.

The resulting hybrid policies now account for four out of every 10 new policies and have made life insurance more competitive. In fact, since under tax changes children's assets are now taxed at a parent's tax rate, some families have been buying life insurance for their children because its annual buildup of cash value isn't taxed for either adults or children. Thus the policy provides a base of investment for a child and an asset against which the child can one day borrow.

Unfortunately, new policies have also meant considerable confusion for the average consumer about actual yields and whether he's buying primarily insurance or an investment. Many of the life policies, which basically combine a guaranteed insurance benefit with a tax-deferred savings account, tout rates much higher than you'll really receive. "Some advertisements don't, for example, point out that the rate can change or already may have changed," said James H. Hunt, director of the National Insurance Consumers Organization in Alexandria, Va., which will do a cost and yield analysis on any policy for a $25 fee. "I saw one trade publication quoting a rate of 11.5 percent on its "universal" life (which permits varying or even discontinuing of premium payments), but the actual rate was closer to 8 percent."

In addition, some companies don't pay interest on the first $1,000 of cash value. Or, they charge you more for the term life insurance protection included to pay a higher investment rate. The advertised return is often a gross rather than a net rate. It isn't adjusted for either sales commissions or administrative fees and also doesn't point out any surrender charge you might have to pay if you cashed in the policy.

Always carefully compare the total costs, return and insurance coverage of several policies if you finally decide to go with universal life rather than simply buy insurance and make investments separately. Though the major switch in the insurance industry has been to universal life, it is not quite as popular in a period in which interest rates are lower. With universal life, you can stop or start your payments whenever you feel like it though certain requirements must be met. While it generally offers only one investment choice, such as a fund that puts money in short-term Treasury securities, a few policies are offering more extensive choices.

It's a good idea to check out the insurance company. A.M. Best Co. publishes an independent rating book, available in most public libraries, which tells the stability of the company, its track record, financial analysis and how the management operates. It has an alphabetical rating system, and many experts advise not buying insurance from any company rated A-minus or less.

Know the differences in basic insurance. Traditional whole life has fixed premiums payable for life and offers steady if not overwhelming dividends. Term insurance is coverage for only a certain period of time, rather than your entire life, with premiums starting low but rising with age. Always shop a number of insurance policies, comparing costs and benefits in each case. If you're a middle-income individual with dependents, it is probable that you'll need life insurance coverage of $100,000 or more. Enough insurance should be bought that were the proceeds invested, one could live off of the interest or income they provide. Look for policies that offer a special deal if you don't smoke or meet other specific criteria. Some may require that you take an extensive physical and you may have to declare in writing that you exercise regularly. By meeting the criteria of various incentives, you can cut your premium in half.

Another new alternative, variable life insurance, has a fixed premium and fixed death benefit and permits you to increase your benefits by investing in stocks, bonds and money market funds, with the ability to switch between funds from time to time. "Our variable life policies invest in the Zenith funds, with both our stock fund and bond fund up significantly last year," said James F. Brogan, vice president with New England Life. "But it is important to keep in mind that these returns may not be so substantial every year, and that your cash value is at risk." (Although the insurance benefit is guaranteed.)

Single-premium whole life insurance policies are the hottest item going in insurance right now, offering high tax-free yields and life insurance as well. Their benefits have not been damaged by tax changes. Earnings accumulate tax-free, though early withdrawal of money would require that all money earned within the policy be taxed. You can borrow against the policy with no tax consequences. With most policies, there's no charge so long as you're borrowing against interest earned inside the policy but not cutting into your original premium deposit. Interest on the loan is offset dollar-for-dollar by interest being credited to the policy. Withdrawal, while it will affect your death benefit, doesn't cost anything and doesn't require repayment. While single-premium policies are insurance, for obvious reasons they are increasingly being sold by brokers touting the return and tax benefits.

Single-premium whole life requires one initial premium and the policy is then paid up. The single premium is usually $25,000 or more, though some are as low as $5,000. The size of the death benefit depends on your age when you buy the policy and can fluctuate depending on how much you borrow from the policy. The insurance firm invests most of the premium for you, and the income compounds tax-free in your account. They typically pay a fixed return for a set duration of up to five years, with rates then readjusted to reflect the market. There's an insurance guarantee against erosion of your principal. Yields are competitive with municipal bonds.

There are also single-premium variable life policies in which the cash value varies with the success of the underlying mutual fund. You may have to pay a charge, however, should you surrender the policy, and you'll owe taxes on earnings you've built up. Make sure you're dealing with an insurance company you can trust, checking out the firm in A.M. Best to make absolutely sure the product you're considering qualifies as life insurance and thus retains the typical life insurance tax benefits. Find out whether the rate of return is a net rate or a gross rate. Some companies give the gross rate without explaining that some of that return will be taken out by the company for its costs.

Single-premium policies should be considered long-term investments because of substantial surrender charges for early cash-in. Apart from tax advantage and investment potential, carefully examine the life insurance that is attached. If your sole goal really is insurance coverage, you may do better buying conventional whole life or term life coverage. Study alternatives, then contact your insurance agent or financial planner. If that agent won't discuss possibilities that might include cutting back coverage or cashing in policies to invest in different policies, consider finding another agent. Remember that your primary goal is providing for dependents. A general rule is to have enough insurance so that your family could invest the proceeds and live off the interest from them.

Another alternative, the single-premium annuity, is basically a tax-deferred retirement saving plan, similar to an IRA with no tax deduction. Money withdrawn in a lump sum or in annuity payments after retirement age is subject to ordinary income tax on the earnings portion, when you'll likely be in a lower income bracket. Some annuities offer a guaranteed interest rate that changes at intervals of from one to three years, while variable annuities permit you to choose among investments such as mutual funds or unit trusts to aim for the best return.

Remember the differences between annuities and life insurance. If the individual has a single-premium deferred annuity and takes money out of it during his lifetime, there will be taxation on interest. In addition, if he takes the money out before age 59½, there will be a 10 percent IRS penalty. But with single-premium life insurance, the individual can get money out of it through policy loans without incurring any current taxation or penalties.

Insurance may be a favored child of the new tax laws, but

keep in mind other long-term considerations for yourself and your family, such as wills and health coverage. Like life insurance, people don't usually like to talk about them.

Seventy percent of Americans die without a will. A reason why many folks never get around to making one is a nagging feeling that the very act of signing it somehow hastens their death. A well-executed will does, however, give you solid control over eventual distribution of your property. It's a good idea for both single and married adults. "Just take care of your will and then go on enjoying your life," advised Conrad Teitell, partner in the New York City law firm of Prerau & Teitell. "Draft it, update it periodically, put it in a safe place. Then don't think about it."

Without a will, effective control of distribution isn't generally possible unless careful use of joint tenancy and trusts has made your estate truly cut-and-dried. Without a will, the state often winds up calling the shots. It doesn't cost a fortune to make a will. One can even be drafted without a lawyer and there are do-it-yourself kits and computer programs that help. However, a lawyer knowledgeable about state statutes can probably best handle the terminology and the proper execution of the document with witnesses. Typical cost of a will for a simple estate is $200 to $300, though some legal chains charge less. For example, Hyatt Legal Services charges $75 for an individual will or $95 for two wills for a couple. The procedure is simple and usually takes about half an hour.

Follow basic steps to make sure your will is an effective one. First, collect information on your assets and liabilities. Financial records should include the deed to your home, car title, insurance policies, bank statements and stock certificates. Make a memorandum of important personal facts, such as addresses, birth dates, Social Security numbers, date and place of marriage and the addresses and ages of beneficiaries. Decide who should receive property and in what amounts. Be precise. Lack of clarity may cause problems for your beneficiaries later. Wills frequently arrange for payment of taxes and funeral and burial expenses, thereby simplifying the probating of the estate and saving added court costs later.

Choose the individual who will be guardian of your children. Otherwise, the court will do so and its preference may not be the same as yours. It could, for example, choose your brother who lives out of state and then move your children there, even though you'd have preferred that they remain in the same city they are now. Consider whether a trust should be created for your spouse, children or others. Trusts can protect your estate against loss or guard against inexperienced handling by heirs.

Be careful in selecting an executor of your will, making sure he is not only willing but able to do the job. If you die without a will, the individual selected by law to serve as executor may be inconvenienced by having to pay for a bond. With a will, you can stipulate that the executor you've chosen needn't furnish bond. Go over designated beneficiaries of life insurance, pensions and individual retirement accounts. Remember that these contracts take precedence over any stipulations in a will.

When drafting the will with the lawyer, be specific, since he will only be as effective as the information you outline for him. Particularly in regard to personal items such as jewelry or furniture, spell everything out. Store the will in a safe place, with the executor or family members knowing where it is and able to get to it. Review it periodically and make changes when appropriate by executing an amendment, known as a codicil, through your lawyer. A fee will be charged for such changes.

No one likes to think about getting sick, but health insurance is a primary consideration for every family.

In fact, you and your family are the targets of a $100 million barrage of television and print ads aimed at getting you to sign up with a health maintenance organization, commonly known as an HMO. The pitches are aggressive. That's because competition is fierce among a multitude of organizations, some of which are unlikely to survive this expensive battle.

Ironically, HMOs, which provide comprehensive medical coverage and service for a fixed prepaid monthly fee, grew at a snail's pace for decades after the opening of the first prototype in Los Angeles in 1929. During the 1980s, as the emphasis upon "containment" of health costs has grown, so have HMOs. The number of Americans enrolled in HMOs leaped by 25 percent in the last year to more than 21 million. "There was only one HMO in Phoenix last year and this year there are 16 of them," said a Tucson HMO executive. "I can guarantee you that in another two years there will be nowhere near that many, for there's going to be an inevitable shakeout in cities across the country."

Your employer probably offers you several choices of coverage and there are many differences, even among each type of plan. Should you keep traditional insurance coverage, the predominant choice, you can have any doctor you choose. You'll most likely receive 80 percent reimbursement, although that percentage is coming down in many plans. On the other hand, with an HMO, 100 percent of expenses are generally covered.

A growing alternative, the preferred provider organization, or PPO, offers financial incentives if you use approved doctors and hospitals. It typically reimburses 90 percent or more if you follow its approved list, but will reimburse to a lesser degree if you choose other care.

Health care is highly personal. For example, a young couple with twins chose traditional coverage because of a close relationship with a trusted doctor. Another couple said they preferred an HMO because they have received excellent care and never need to hestitate to take their children to the doctor for financial reasons. "Our HMO took over everything and did all the paperwork," said Genevieve Vatter of Willowbrook, Ill., whose colon cancer was discovered during preventive testing by her HMO and operated upon successfully. "Everything was totally covered."

HMOs get high marks from most members. However, a recently-released study by Rand Corp., a Santa Monica, Calif.-based think tank, of a group of Seattle patients over a five-year period found that patients had greater satisfaction with fee-for-service medicine because of availability of specialists and hospitals, shorter waits for appointments and better relationships between patient and doctor. Fifteen percent of the assigned HMO group were dissatisfied with their care, compared with 10 percent of enrollees in traditional programs. A Harris poll conducted for the HMO-affiliated Kaiser Family Foundation found that the general satisfaction with medical care among HMO patients has suffered a drop during the 1980s.

Of course, there are difference in HMOs in quality, length of office waits, ability to see certain physicians and likelihood that the HMO will be around long-term. Visit several and also talk to members. In one case, a woman complained that her HMO treated her like a number and sent her far outside her neighborhood when she needed a specialist. Benefits administrators say that, because of HMO telephone screen procedures, a member usually has to be firm in requesting an appointment with a doctor. "Remember that HMOs make profits by not seeing people," said Robert Bonin, manager of benefits adminstration for First Chicago Corp. "If the HMO sees a member as often as the member wants, it won't make money."

When considering traditional coverage, ask yourself: Do you want a specific doctor? Do you want no restrictions? Can you afford coverage? Will you receive preventive care? Do you travel frequently or have a child in school out of state? (An HMO won't cover out-of-state treatment unless it has a reciprocal agreement with a group in that city.)

When considering an HMO, ask: What services are included? What choice will you have in physicians? What is the quality of the affiliated hospital? What is the history of the HMO and turnover rate of its doctors? How convenient is it to where you live? Are special features, such as weight-loss or stop-smoking classes, offered?

When considering a PPO, ask: Is it available from your employer? Is your current doctor a member? How much will you save versus traditional coverage? What is the hospital affiliation?

9   Credit Cop-out

Americans have a loaded gun pointed at their credit cards. It's the new tax law, which gradually phases out deductions for interest over five years.

Painful as it may be, this is exactly what some folks needed. The stories of credit misuse are legion.

For example, a budget was being worked out for a client by a financial planner, carefully going over each and every detail of daily living expenses. But after perusing the information supplied, the adviser noticed no allotment for spending on clothing. "You'll really have to realistically figure on spending some money on clothes this year," the planner said.

The client shook her head. "No need to," she said with a shrug. "I charge all my clothes."

In another case, a man deeply in credit card debt actually came to a session with a credit counsellor holding in his hand a brown paper bag filled to the top with unpaid billings. "Please, you do it," he pleaded as he handed the bag over to the counsellor. "I just can't bear to look any more."

A highly-paid professional couple that I know pays for virtually everything with credit cards. A $2 drink after work, if the establishment won't accept plastic for such a small amount, or a cab fare always mean borrowing a few greenbacks from those around them. Cash just isn't a part of their lives.

As sophisticated as the American consumer has become, many people still don't think of credit cards as money. Apart from the unacceptability of carrying such debt in a new tax system in which one can no longer deduct the interest, there is also the fact that the return on basic investments is low these days, making high-interest debt even more onerous.

But many Americans don't shop for the best rates or discipline themselves in the use of their cards. The card is simply plastic "funny money." You can handle your cards better, and you can also likely find lower interest rates than you're now paying. Credit card rates never move down as quickly as rates on savings do during general periods of lower rates, and it's not hard to figure out why. They're big moneymakers for the institutions offering them. Unfortunately, they're big money losers for millions of Americans. A $1,000 balance, allowed to revolve at 21 percent, will cost $210 in finance charges over a year. At 19.8 percent, it is still $198, while a 17.8 percent charge comes out to $178. Any shopping for a good savings return can be wiped out by such excessive card charges.

"Financial institutions are keeping rates so high because they see people don't use restraint with their cards," said U.S. Rep. Frank Annunzio (D., Ill.), who as chairman of the House Consumer Affairs and Coinage Subcommittee has held hearings on high card rates. Rep. Charles E. Shumer (D, N.Y.), in seeking a ceiling on credit interest, said "billions of dollars is being spent every year on unjustified credit costs."

About a third of all cardholders never pay any interest because they pay off their monthly balance in full. The rest allow their credit to revolve, which is fine so long as they handle it sensibly. It's often a good idea for a consumer to keep only one or two credit cards in his or her wallet, except when making a pre-planned purchase, thus lessening temptation. Never buy groceries with a card, since that is not the intended use. No one should be paying high finance charges on food. Try to avoid impulse charging. During the holiday season, for example, it's often a good idea to come up with a basic budget beforehand for how much should be spent on various gifts. At the end of each shopping trip, sit down and add up the sales slips to see if the budget was met.

If you do run into problems paying off your credit card debt, don't run away from the problem. Try to talk it through with your creditors, explaining why there have been late payments and letting them know that you intend to make good on your debts. Perhaps a credit counsellor, who will help you consolidate your debts into fewer payments, can help you discipline yourself to meeting your commitments. "It was an absolute mess, with me living in total fear, and then charging more to try to make myself feel better," said one woman, who successfully worked her way out of her problems with a counsellor. "There were endless phone calls at home and work from department stores and lawyers, and it wasn't until I stopped running away and tried to do something about it that things improved and I got back on track."

In daily use of your credit cards, card safety is also important. Compare your sales slips to the actual charges billed. You may find that someone has changed numbers. Be sure to get your credit card back after each transaction, since a stolen card can easily be sold on the open market. Make sure that when a salesperson makes a mistake in filling out a slip that he or she actually tears up the slip. Some employees have been known to use the blank slip to purchase items on the customer's tab.

The big banks blanketing the country with their credit card marketing campaigns aren't the ones offering the best rates. These financial giants are primarily pushing frills, such as travel and entertainment benefits, through their flashy mailings and advertisements. Interest charges and annual fees the consumer will wind up paying are often obscured in the fine print of application forms. The high rates and fees are the obvious reason why.

While flash does sell, a growing number of Americans have figured out the high price they're paying to use credit cards.

Savvy credit-watchers are seeking out the best deals. At the very least, this should mean shopping among four or five local financial institutions to compare rates and annual fees. For those who are really serious, it might mean looking for a card from a rate-conscious out-of-state institution. This requires contacting the bank for an application and going through the same credit check you'd undergo at a local institution. "We've been dealing with a public misconception that all fees and interest rates are alike, plus the mistaken belief that credit cards from smaller or out-of-state banks aren't as widely accepted," said Elgie Holstein, associate director of the nonprofit Bankcard Holders of America in Washington, D.C. "The fact is, the location of the bank where you have your credit card doesn't really make a difference any more."

Arkansas, generally the leader in low credit rates, has a constitutional provision setting the ceilings at 5 percent above the federal discount rate. Simmons First National Bank, P.O. Box 6609, Pine Bluff, Ark. 71611, in late 1986 was offering a rate of 10.5 percent, with a $22.50 annual fee and 25-day grace period for payment. "I think real recognition of lower rate cards began in 1986 and we've seen our total number of Visa and MasterCard customers increase by 30 percent," said Tom Paxton, vice president with Simmons First National Bank. "Out-of-state people write or telephone us about cards and we simply have them fill out an application, with the issuing of cards based on our normal criteria." Union National Bank, P.O. Box 1541, Little Rock, Ark. 72203, was also charging 10.5 percent, but starts charging interest immediately with each purchase and exacts a $20 annual fee. Removal of card restrictions in Connecticut resulted in a rate war, with Connecticut National Bank, 777 Main St., Hartford, Conn. 06115, offering an 11.75 percent card with 25-day grace period and $25 annual fee.

The nudge toward lower credit card rates is being accelerated by a number of groups, such as credit unions, college alumni associations and even the National Rifle Association. They're offering their own discount cards to members. For example, the AFL-CIO, in conjunction with Bank of New York, is offering two MasterCard plans. One has a rate 5 percentage points above the prime lending rate with no annual fee and no grace period. The other option is a rate 7.25 percentage points above prime, no annual fee until the second year and 25-day grace period. Initially offered to union members, there are plans to make the card available to nonunion workers who sign up for an "associate" membership.

You must look carefully even at low rates, however. Some banks, rather than offering the usual full-month grace period before payment is due, start charging interest immediately, as soon as purchases are made. If you normally pay off your bill in full each month, you're much better off with a card that has a grace period. However, if you typically permit your monthly balance to revolve, you'll do better with a lower-rate card because interest charges should be your primary concern. Whatever the deal being offered, always read the fine print.

The Bankcard Holders of America, 333 Pennsylvania Ave. S.E., Washington, D.C., 20003 ranks the best credit card deals and provides lists of them on request. For $1, it offers a list of 30 banks with the lowest credit card interest rates. For $1.98, it provides a list of banks with no annual card fees.

While there are obvious drawbacks to credit card use, it has become more difficult to survive financially without those shiny pieces of plastic. That's because, aside from their convenience, credit cards are a record of financial stability and an initial foundation for any major borrowing you'll be doing throughout your life.

Many Americans, whether graduating from school or already on the job, don't really know how to establish credit or maintain a long-term credit rating. They may hold responsible positions, but seem to get rejected out of hand or never really figure out what the credit process is all about. The best way to make the initial move is to start small and keep trying. A typical first loan is a car loan, which is easier to get because it is secured by the value of the car itself. Next, move on to a small department store to get a credit card, since it may not have the same hard-and-fast credit-granting rules as big banks. Or start out by opening even a modest checking or savings account at your local bank and handle it well. Once you have $500 in the bank, you can ask for a credit card and use the money in the bank as collateral. "Another ideal starting point might be a small loan of $1,000 or so for a vacation trip," advised Kenneth B. Herz, vice president with New York's Chemical Bank. "Pay it off on time and the bank should be impressed and willing to offer you other credit."

In addition, make sure you have a solid payment record with the companies that provide your utilities, because that small factor could make a big difference in whether you're granted credit. Don't fear credit information bureaus, but instead be aware of what they are all about. The information they gather consists of three separate areas:

—Name, address, Social Security number and date of birth.

—The account section, which lists where you have accounts, such as banks, department stores and finance companies. It explains whether the account is revolving or installment, the credit limits, the current balance and whether you have any late bills outstanding.

—The public record information, which includes tax liens, judgments and bankruptcy records.

Credit reporting companies, such as TRW, Trans Union, Equifax, Chilton Corp. or Pinger, give only a report and not a rating. Check your yellow pages for the one that covers your region. Final decision is made by the individual bank or department store, which also takes into account additional information such as how long you've held your job and lived at your current address. In the case of people who haven't held credit accounts, a simple "no report" is issued by the credit agency.

You can usually get a copy of your individual report for $10 or less by mailing a letter including your name, address, Social Security number, date of birth and signature with a statement that you'd like a copy of your report. If you dispute some information, the agency will check out the data. If you're proved correct, the incorrect information will be purged from your file. If the information is kept as is and you disagree, you may place a 100-word statement in your own file. The credit agency will help write the statement, if you wish. Credit rating agencies say bankruptcy stays on the credit record for a full 10 years, while other types of negative information stay for seven years. Yet some agencies don't bother to remove information about a past loan in default or a past bankruptcy. Some include a continuing notation, and the inclusion of such information on your report is not considered an illegal act.

Get credit when credit is due, but from now on, realize that carrying large credit balances just doesn't make sense under the new tax laws. You can't make money if you're losing money on credit cards.

10 Taking Stock

Stocks are "in" under the new tax laws, but you have to avoid simply running with the herd.

A financial journalist, so the story goes, was covering a stockbroker convention in Florida which was studying the effects of the tax laws. During the second day of meetings, an enormous hurricane whipped through the convention hall. All in attendance were killed immediately and swept up to heaven. Moments later, the journalist found himself at the end of a long line of brokers in pin-striped suits. St. Peter was explaining to everyone that only a limited number of passes were available that day to enter the Pearly Gates.

Quickly sizing up the situation, the inventive journalist stepped onto a soapbox lying nearby. "Immediate opportunities in new-issue and utility stocks in a recently-opened branch brokerage office in Hell!" he shouted. "Lucrative prospects for self-starters willing to relocate!"

The brokers looked over their shoulders as they heard those enticing words. After brief hesitation, one by one they turned and began barreling toward the Stairway to Hell. Dozens ran pell-mell into the abyss. The journalist hesitated for a moment, then himself began running toward the stairway.

St. Peter, stunned by what he had seen transpire, called to

the journalist as he headed toward the fiery stairwell: "What are you doing? You're the one who started all of this!" The journalist yelled over his shoulder as he entered the stairwell: "Who knows? There just might be something to the tip!"

While the herd instinct may be a big part of Wall Street in these days of tax law changes, it's best to confront the market as a thinking individual. Yes, the stock market and other financial instruments should look more attractive under the new tax laws. High-dividend stocks of all types may look particularly good in an environment of lower individual tax brackets. Some companies may even be increasing dividends at a more rapid pace in the future. But your decisions should be your own, based upon your individual situation.

It's worth noting that the interest on borrowing to make an investment, such as the increasingly popular practice of buying stocks on margin, retains its tax-deductibility under the new laws, but with some restrictions.

You'll be permitted to deduct these interest costs only up to the amount of investment income—including dividends, interest income and capital gains. In the past, you could deduct such investment interest up to an amount $10,000 more than your investment income. That $10,000 umbrella is phased out so that by 1991, you can only deduct investment interest up to your investment income. This new cap applies to interest paid starting in 1987, no matter when the debt was initially incurred. Interest that is disallowed can be carried forward to offset future investment income. The limit is phased in so that 65 percent of the $10,000 umbrella is still deductible in 1987, 40 percent in 1988, 20 percent in 1989, 10 percent in 1990 and none in 1991. At the same time, Wall Street firms are increasingly using the margin account for more general purpose loans, based upon other investments held with the brokerage firm. (There will be more on the pros and cons of investing on margin later in this chapter.)

For some stock investors, the first time's a charm. Their initial foray into the stock market still provides sweet dreams of a well-played hunch or friendly tip that led to pleasing results.

They talk about it a lot. Yet for other investors, that earliest shot at risk-taking conjures up recurring nightmares of paychecks wasted on losing propositions. This is usually a much quieter group of folks. Between these two camps is the broad mainstream of would-be investors. They perk up when they hear of an impressive stock market rally or individual tales of trading triumph, but they aren't really sure they're ready for that first walk down Wall Street. After all, they ask, doesn't that program-trading stuff wipe out all your gains?

A good start is investing in four or five stocks, each selling for around $25 per share and bought in quantities of 100 shares. Since individual stocks perform differently at various times, a diversified portfolio helps spread out those ups and downs more evenly. Hundred-share lots are considered the norm and buying fewer shares than that will result in a greater charge per share. Select some investment goals.

If you'd like steady dividends and your tax bracket is low enough to permit them, invest in regional telephone stocks, non-nuclear electric utility stocks or other blue-chips that don't bring surprises. Strong dividends are definitely in vogue under the new tax laws.

The electric utility stock, for example, has been crowned one of the likely beneficiaries of tax changes, thanks to its traditional high dividends. But these utilities have already been providing a lot more kick for investors than dividends alone. They've handily outperformed the market in overall return, with considerable price appreciation a part of that. In addition, the staid world of utilities is now entering an era of takeovers, with some experts predicting that the 150 companies currently in existence will drop to about 50 during the rest of the 1980s and cause a lot of price action in their stocks. Most electric utilities are in excellent financial shape, since they're no longer involved in the massive and controversial nuclear construction projects of the past few years. While the loss of the investment tax credit will hurt some involved in construction and also some of the smaller utilities, right now that isn't significant. With low interest rates, electric utilities look like good bets for investors who benefit from lower tax brackets. Remember that the higher the dividend a utility offers, the greater risk the investor must be willing to assume.

If you'd like to try for some positive surprises and are much more willing to assume risk than your more conservative brethren, go with emerging smaller companies that won't have significant dividends to add to your tax bite. They're often sold on the over-the-counter market rather than on the major exchanges and are more volatile in price.

If you don't have that kind of money right now, you might invest in a stock mutual fund requiring an initial outlay of $1,000 or less. When you get enough money, head for the market itself. Remember that you could lose all of the money you invest. Don't play the market to come up with funds needed for mortgage payments or the kids' tuition, because the value of stocks can come down just when you need those dollars the most. Don't be a child-like investor. Don't base all decisions on your broker or friends. Read financial publications and your daily newspaper business section and request research reports and other investment information from your broker. Put together your own small research library at home so you'll keep up on events. You don't necessarily need a home computer to keep track of your investments; pencil and paper will do just fine.

If your broker (or, if the more stylish term is preferred, financial consultant) initially isn't interested in a smaller investor, it's unlikely that attitude will change. Take your business—and potential commissions—elsewhere. The relationship with the customer can be one of close friendship or intense distrust. They may talk frequently or rarely. They may be teacher and pupil, or battling adversaries, each convinced they know the best use of investment cash. Be candid about the amount of money you are willing to invest and how active you wish your account to be. A broker who has been informed that you wish a stable, conservative portfolio will be less likely to call you with every hot new tip. Similarly, if you have told your broker you are willing to accept some risks, the two of you can communicate regularly to take advantage of changing opportunities.

Talk over how often you may be likely to ask for specific price quotes. If there is activity in a stock and conditions are changing rapidly, frequent price quotes should be no problem. But if you telephone simply out of routine or nervousness, you may be cutting into time your broker could better spend going over his firm's research or otherwise monitoring the market. Don't be offended if an administrative assistant gives you the price quotes you need, since this is often the most efficient way. Don't allow yourself to be pressed or bullied. After all, it is your money. If you feel that you need a bit more time to decide, take it. If you weren't confident about making a snap decision, you probably made the best decision by waiting. There will be other deals in the future. Never look to anyone as your total investment guru. Neither you nor your adviser should shoulder all the blame or take all of the credit. Of course, investors aren't faultless either. "Greed is definitely a big problem as people set a goal, reach it and then immediately say they want more," commented one broker. "A client has to set a mental stop when he or she has gotten a profit, and a broker has to sense that point also."

Discount brokers offer trades at considerably lower cost than full-service brokers, in some cases half the price. Offering no advice on investments, as full-service brokers do, they simply handle transactions. They're available not only at investment firms, but increasingly at banks and savings and loans as well. But before you do it yourself, you'd better know what you're doing. Discount houses sprang into existence a decade ago when the Securities and Exchange Commission abolished the 183-year-old practice of fixing commission rates. They gained momentum in the 1980s, particularly as the government dropped restrictions on banks. Often they are connected to money market mutual funds for ease of purchase and transfer of funds.

While full-service brokers offering investment advice usually do not have a minimum commission charge, discount brokerages do. Finding the least expensive discount broker is not an easy task, for charges vary with the transaction and each discounter's scale is slightly different from the other's. It is important to get a price based on the specific buying or selling that you wish to do, or the type of transactions you'd be most likely to make with a discount firm if you intend to open an ongoing account.

For example, full-service broker Merrill Lynch & Co. has no minimum charge and on a purchase of 100 shares at $25 apiece would require $78.25 in commissions. On 200 shares at $50, the commission would be $192, while 500 shares of a $10 stock would exact $164.50.

Among discount firms, Fidelity Brokerage Services, 161 Devonshire St., Boston, Mass. 02109, (800) 225-1799, has a minimum $33 charge. On a purchase of 100 shares at $25, Fidelity would require $44, on 200 shares at $50 the charge is $88 and on 500 shares at $10 it is $68. Meanwhile, Charles Schwab & Co., 101 Montgomery St., San Francisco, Calif. 94104, (800) 648-5300, has a $34 minimum. For 100 shares at $25 it charges $49, for 200 shares at $50 it requires $92 and for 500 shares at $10 it charges $74.

Several other discounters also show differences. Quick & Reilly Inc., 120 Wall St., New York, N.Y. 10005, (800) 221-5220, has a minimum of $35 and on 100 shares at $25 apiece would charge $35, on 200 shares at $50 would charge $90 and on 500 shares at $10 would require $46. Rose & Co., 440 S. LaSalle St., Suite 3100, Chicago, Ill. 60605, (800) 621-3700, has a minimum of $35 and on a purchase of 100 shares at $25 charges $40, on 200 shares at $50 requires $80 and on 500 shares at $10 charges $65.

Though some advertisements depict the buying of stocks as a rote task quickly learned by some sort of osmosis, there's more to it than that. "People who don't know too much about the stock market simply won't be comfortable with a discount brokerage acount," said an executive with a major discount house. "A basic knowledge of how the market works is absolutely necessary." The hand-holding of a broker is needed by many people plunking their money into the stock market for the first time. Not all brokers provide that, but an ideal broker carefully chosen is often the best way to start out. In addition, many first-time investors don't exactly know the proper terminology involved in trades, and can make an error in ordering with a busy discount trader who is actively grinding out many trades during the day.

Many discount brokerage clients assume all orders telephoned in are tape-recorded by the firm so it can be determined who was at fault if anything goes wrong. Yet, for a variety of reasons, those tapes are not always running, and a difference of opinion on an order could well come down to the client's word against that of the firm.

Learn as much as you can before you invest. Investment clubs provide an excellent way to learn about high finance without having to endanger your family's life savings in the process. There's always a distinct personality to each neighborhood club, whether it has existed for years or was spawned by the most recent interest in the stock market. Some seem like poker night with the boys; others are more like PTA meetings; still others resemble hard-driving corporate board sessions. "In just the last week, I've gotten five telephone calls from people of a variety of ages interested in starting clubs," said Peggy Schmeltz of Bowling Green, Ohio, a longtime member of three separate clubs and a regional officer of the National Association of Investment Clubs. "One trend of the last few years involves clubs made up of women whose husbands have passed away, who want to learn now about investments what they probably should have learned years ago."

Investment clubs, which pool money for stock purchases, usually start with a few friends discussing where they'd invest their money. They become more formalized as members set regular meetings and require a monthly membership contribution to the pot. A typical monthly investment is $25 per member, and club size is usually about 20 members. Some clubs pay occasional dividends to their members from the investments. Club members research potential stock picks, then put to a vote what purchases will be made. Some clubs use advisers; others go it alone. Most read a lot and follow investment reports such as the Value Line Investment Survey and Standard & Poor's Outlook. A great many members are novices there to learn, not to strike it rich. Still, there are successes. Schmeltz, who is a member of one club of men and women investors from around the country, another of senior women from her town and still another of college faculty wives, can tick off a number of stock selections that were profitable last year.

The 6,000-club National Association of Investment Clubs provides information on starting a club and, through its national membership program, continuing support and investor materials as well. Fees for membership are $30 a year per club, plus $7 per member. Club dues include a fidelity bond, which covers the club if one of its members makes off with the money, and a monthly magazine. The group's address is NAIC, 1515 E. Eleven Mile Rd., Royal Oak, Mich. 48067.

The give and take of investment selection isn't always a warm and friendly process, since clubs must often deal with diverse personalities. "The conflicts usually arise when members don't have similar goals, with some wanting to actively get in and out of the market and others seeking to hold long term," noted Thomas E. O'Hare, chairman of the board of trustees of the NAIC and a member of a Detroit group called the Mutual Investment Club, which has been around 47 years. The club, unlike most groups, is big business. For example, when one member who had invested $8,400 over a number of years with the club died recently, the payout to his family was an amazing $254,000.

Seven years ago, when the Glenview, Ill., Senior Women's Investment Club was formed, the founding women members gave local men an opportunity to join. They opted instead to start their own, because they had more confidence in their selections. "The women's group wound up doing better, because the women were more patient and didn't get all excited and sell as quickly as the men did," admitted Robert Lynch, president of the men's group and an adviser to the women's group. "But this past year, both groups did pretty well."

Many investors become interested in the stock market simply because they've found an old certificate or have inherited some stock. Their interest piqued by all the constant talk about the stock market in the news, Americans have been heading for their attics and closets. They're searching through the cobwebs and dust of old trunks in an attempt to dig out their families' almost-forgotten, yellowing stock certificates that—who knows—might actually be worth something.

Chances are, the certificates are virtually worthless. However, there have been some success stories:

—A woman in Largo, Fla., discovered that her 10 shares of Utility Equities Corp., bought in 1930, were worth $560. That corporate name was changed four times before finally being merged into what is now Allied-Signal Inc.

—A man in Inverness, Fla., learned that the North European Oil stock certificates left him by his father five decades ago are worth $40,000. That American company doing business in Germany closed down completely in 1943, but was reopened in 1957 after oil was discovered on its properties.

"About 40 percent of the stock certificates we research turn out to have value of some sort," explained Paul Bonneau, chief researcher of certificates for Stock Market Information Service, based in Montreal. "Some have cash value right now, others have potential cash value if the company regroups and still others have value to collectors based on their artwork, historical importance or scarcity." For example, I.O.S. Ltd. mutual fund shares issued in the 1960s and early 1970s were kept in limbo for 14 years amid scandal and a legal battle over bankruptcy, yet are now worth 60 percent of face value, he said. An 1866 American Express stock certificate is worth $1,000 largely because it bears the signatures of Henry Wells and William Fargo, founders of Wells Fargo.

The outside chance that the certificate you've uncovered is

worth something probably makes doing some resesrch worthwhile. To do it yourself, use the financial section of the local
library, looking back in history through publications of
Moody's Investors Service, Standard & Poor's or the Robert
D. Fisher manual. Check with the secretary of state's office
from which the charter for the company was issued in order
to obtain the most basic information on the company. Pick the
brains of local stockbrokers who may remember what happened to that company whose unfamiliar name is on your
certificate. If you still turn up a blank you can turn to a research firm, which does this sort of sleuthing every day. "We
start by looking through our files, some of which have been
in existence 100 years, then write the necessary letters to get
the full facts," said Diane Herzog, vice president of R.M.
Smythe & Co., which has been doing searches since the firm
was started in 1880 by Irish immigrant Roland Smythe.

It usually takes three to six weeks for companies to complete
the research. In truly difficult and convoluted searches, this
can stretch for many months. Stock Market Information Service, P.O. Box 120, Station K, Montreal, Canada, H1N 3K9,
charges $50 per company researched, plus 20 percent of the
value of the stocks if they turn out to be worth more than
$2,000, 30 percent if less than $2,000. It handles the money
recovery, including assuming of expenses in the case of legal
entanglements. R.M. Smythe & Co., 24 Broadway, New York,
N.Y., 10004, charges a flat $25 fee for each research report. It
doesn't do actual recovery of money unless asked to do so,
in which case it charges according to the hours required. Stock
Market Information Service was born quite by accident 21
years ago when Micheline Masse, its president, was wallpa-
pering a room in her home with stock certificates donated by
friends. She did a little research and, to her surprise, found
that one certificate was worth $5,000. She gave it back, but,
fascinated by her discovery, decided to turn certificate
searches into a business.

For the average stock investor, the big worry isn't so much
keeping up with an old stock that's been lost as it is figuring

out what's happening with stocks he's bought and is trying
to follow closely.

One major way of tracking involves the annual reports of
the companies whose stock he holds or is considering buying.
The annual reports mailed to millions of shareholders each
year represent the finest creative writing of corporate America.
Don't be dazzled by bright colors, elaborate graphics or fancy
prose. What matters is what the company does, whether it
made money for you last year and what its game plan for
success will be this year.

Several years ago, I was judging a competition that pitted
dozens of annual reports against each other. One entry from
a major bank printed several shiny pages of its financial
figures in a deep turqoise hue that all but obscured the black
type.

"This report looks terrific, really beautiful," a fellow judge
said.

"I can't read a thing through all this blue," I complained.

"Looks great against the skyline shot on the next page,
though," he persisted. "To do it any differently would have
ruined the cropping of the picture."

Sorry, I'll still take good old readable black-on-white any
day.

It's often a good idea to start out by reading the detail in
the back of the report, not the public relations effort up front.
Footnotes frequently contain key information the company
doesn't want to emphasize. A change in accounting procedure
or shift in assets mentioned in one sentence can mean more
than paragraphs elsewhere. In the latest batch of annual reports, banks are revealing more detail as to their loan exposure
and overall quality of assets, important information that isn't
in the regular balance sheet, noted one Wall Street analyst.
The chief executive's letter is one of the parts of a report that
isn't dictated by the government. It allows the top executive
to explain his philosophy, which could have far-reaching effects. Also look at the auditor's opinion and make sure it is

an unqualified opinion, meaning that the auditors agree with management.

The amount that companies spend on a single copy of an annual report ranges from 39 cents to more than $5. Investors must also be on the lookout for tricks companies use to make themselves look better, such as neglecting to include in the financial figures a column that gives percentage changes.

An annual report's figures consist basically of (1) a balance sheet that logs year-end assets and liabilities and (2) an income statement comparing income from sales and investments to the costs required to run the company. When reading the balance sheet, note the difference between current assets and current liabilities. That difference is the net working capital, the money the company has to allow it to grow. Also important is stockholder equity, or net worth, usually shown on a per-share basis. It will determine the book value of the stock, and can also effect the price the stockholder is likely to get for it. Watch for undue increases in either the accounts receivable (what people owe the company) or inventories (the materials and goods held by the business). Most important under liabilities is accounts payable, the money the company owes for basic needs such as raw materials and supplies.

The income statement will explain how net sales and operating cost have fared compared with previous years. Trends in the margins of profit, a figure obtained by dividing net income by net assets, is important. Keep in mind that annual reports also are 'report cards' of corporate America that include social policy concerns such as the environment, which could determine whether it's the type of company you want to invest in.

As an investor, be on the outlook for any deals that might make it easier to buy stock and build up your holdings. For example, dividend reinvestment plans may not get much publicity these days, but they're definitely alive and kicking.

These plans permit millions of Americans to automatically plow their dividends into the buying of additional company shares. There are no brokerage fees and, in some cases, there's a discount on the price of those shares purchased as well. More than 600 U.S. firms offer dividend reinvestment plans, providing plenty of choice for the average investor. In addition, cash contributions can usually be made to the plan at regular intervals. For example, one-third of all AT&T share holders, or nearly 3 million people, reinvest their dividends to buy new shares. One-third of all McDonald's Corp. shareholders, or 10,000 investors, do the same. "The reinvestment plan makes shareholders happy and lets the company raise additional capital with very little trouble," said Bruce Barr, director of investor relations for AT&T. "Dividend and cash contributions through our plan generate about $80 million each quarter."

It can pay off. At Central and South West, an electric utility based in Dallas, a $1,500 investment in 100 shares of the firm's stock in 1979, with dividends reinvested, would have grown by now to 247 shares worth more than $8,000. Many investors view the dividend reinvestment plans primarily as a convenience, much like a payroll deduction plan. Buying small amounts of shares would normally be made too expensive because of commission charges. The drawback is that having the money tied up in a dividend reinvestment plan could slow your ability to sell shares in a hurry.

Wally Rogers, 62, a textile sales representative from Highland Park, Ill., first got personally involved in dividend reinvestment plans a couple of years ago and has become a devout believer. He was looking for a handy savings vehicle and considered the stock of telephone companies and electric utilities to be underpriced. So he purchased shares of Ameritech, AT&T, New York State Electric & Gas and Ohio Edison and joined their respective investment plans. "These are a painless way to buy small quantities of stock without brokerage fees," Rogers explained. To join a dividend reinvestment program, a shareholder must first ask if it is available at a company he's interested in. Request an enrollment card. The company's designated transfer agent will reinvest all or some of your regular dividends as requested. Remember that you must pay income tax on reinvested dividends each year, just as if you had received a cash dividend. A number of firms permit investors to buy shares at 3 to 5 percent discounts, though that number is steadily dwindling. When buying shares at a discount, the amount of the discount is taxable income.

Investors in public utilities had been permitted to defer tax on up to $1,500 a year in reinvested dividends. When that opportunity expired, a number of shareholders dropped out. Another drawback of reinvestment plans is that, particularly with companies offering small dividends, it takes quite a while to buy many shares. That's precisely why McDonald's permits cash contributions of $20 to $1,000 per month and AT&T has raised its maximum quarterly investment from $3,000 to $5,000. No one expects a boom in dividend reinvestment plans, but they should keep chugging along, no matter what happens. "Tax reform shouldn't affect reinvestment plans at all, since the main benefit will still be the lack of brokerage fees and that won't change," added Barr of AT&T. "It'll still be a disciplined savings plan offering appreciation and yield."

The stock market is much more volatile these days than in the past, making a lot of investors wary of shelling out their hard-earned dollars. One reason is what's known as "program trading."

The third Fridays of March, June, September and December are the "triple-witching" days when contracts for stock index options and futures and individual stock options all expire at once. Those days are likely to have the most market volatility, because of high-volume computerized trading by major pension funds and investment firms. Massive buy and sell orders kicked in automatically by computer have not only helped send the stock market to record highs, but had a hand in dramatic declines as well. They can exaggerate the good or bad on any given day.

Program trading, say many Wall Streeters, exaggerates a mood, especially a strong mood, and contributes to instability in the market. They fear it may be scaring a lot of Americans away from individual stocks and into stock mutual funds instead.

The average investor can't participate in program trading. But he could wind up with a big loss by getting in on the wrong side of such moves in which institutions buy stocks and sell futures short, or buy futures and sell stocks short. (Some observers believe investors should even be somewhat cautious about investing on the third Friday of every month, when options contracts expire, though the record doesn't indicate the same degree of disruption.)

"The intelligent investor should obviously keep in mind the potential for a change in the market, so those days are worth noting," said William J. Brodsky, president and chief executive officer of the Chicago Mercantile Exchange. "However, just because a phenomenon can be identified doesn't mean that the products involved are not serving a useful purpose."

Spokesmen at the Chicago Board Options Exchange add that investors in the market must simply adjust to the possibility of swings of 35 points or more on a given day, because market averages are at higher levels and large trades are a fact of life. "In addition, for protection, the individual buying stock can use options himself by buying a put (which gives the right to sell stock at a set price for a set period of time)," said Robert A. Bassi, vice president with the CBOE.

Stock-index options and futures permit investors to hedge or speculate on the direction of the stock market. An option on a stock index permits an investor to buy or sell a quoted value of the index for a set price during a specified period. A future on a stock index is a commitment to buy or sell a quoted value of the index at a set price at a set time. Both stock-index futures and options settle in cash, without the underlying stocks changing hands. As far as average investors are concerned, brokers say more of them use strategies such as options than one might expect.

When investing in the stock market, many Americans look for the possibility of a takeover and making a killing on one's stock. Just remember that a takeover deal doesn't always mean a sweet deal for shareholders.

It's true that big-buck deals such as the General Electric offer for RCA Corp., the R.J. Reynolds purchase of Nabisco and the Capital Cities acquisition of ABC put smiles on shareholder faces. But numerous bids for companies fail, the stock slipping back as a result. Other companies, such as Godfather's Pizza, were bought out for less than the price at which their stock was trading. "Every rumor has a different level of quality and every deal is different, so it's difficult for a shareholder to react," said Neil R. Feldman, vice president with Argus Research Corp. "And while cash tender offers usually take four to six weeks, investors should realize that hostile takeovers or deals that encounter financing difficulties may linger for months."

The investor must decide whether to sell as the stock price rises, or stick it out to the end of a deal. If the difference is just a few dollars a share, many experts suggest that you take the money and run. "Should you find your stock in takeover rumors or a takeover, I recommend taking profits after a significant price rise, not waiting," advised Carl Schrager, editor of the *Weekly Takeover Target* newsletter, Santa Barbara, Calif. "A lot can go wrong with deals, and this way you also get use of your money sooner."

Here are the possibilities an investor may encounter:

—*Takeovers*. The investor finds his stock moving up in price as an aggressor takes off after the company, and competing bids may drive the stock price up further. Should the deal be consummated, the investor will be paid in straight cash or with a package that includes stocks or bonds of the takeover company. However, management may chase away the raider of pay him off to go away, moves that could end the deal or even endanger the company's financial strength. Quite often the price goes higher than the offering price because people expect a white knight company to make another bid. Unfortunately, sometimes that knight never appears.

—*Leveraged buyouts*. This proposal by a firm's management or an investor group to take the company private is accomplished by offering to purchase outstanding shares at a premium over current price. The group usually borrows against the company's assets and cash flow to fund the purchase. Always remember that a number of buyouts fall through.

—*Spinoffs*. When a firm decides to unload a subsidiary by making it an independent company, shareholders usually receive stock in the new company on the basis of their holdings in the parent firm. The combination will be approximately equal to the investor's current holdings. Always take a careful look at both firms once the spinoff is consummated to see whether the shares are still worth holding.

Sometimes you must simply back up the truck and sell some of your stocks that aren't performing the way you'd like them to, or have fulfilled all the expectations you had in the first place for them. Though it can be psychologically wrenching to dump any long-time investment, all your financial commitments should regularly undergo the same tough scrutiny that Wall Street gives its recommendations. You should examine all financial commitments on a regular basis, whether they be stocks, certificates of deposit, municipal bonds, mutual funds or even your current mortgage. Yesterday's good idea can be today's mistake.

You have to apply the same discipline to selling that you did to buying, because people typically come up with dozens of reasons to hold on. Don't delay selling until you have every last bit of news about a stock's decline. It may take a long time to figure out the real reason for its slide, and waiting that long could be financially fatal. Never sell based solely upon the outlook for an industry, because each stock has its own individual characteristics. No one should sell simply at the urging of a broker seeking a commission, either.

Ask these questions of every investment when deciding whether to sell:

> — Does it still offer the same potential that it did on the day I initially invested?
>
> — Has it already fulfilled the objective for which I committed my money?

— Have either its upward movement or general benefits slowed down at all?

— Could I confidently recommend this investment now to a close friend?

— Am I unwilling to admit failure and go on to something else?

Another way to get involved in the stock market is trading on margin, the purchase of stocks with borrowed funds, which has reached record levels in recent months.

Your broker will lend you half the money needed, a ratio established by the Federal Reserve Board, thereby doubling your investing power. It is a sweet deal during a bullish market period of onward and upward movement, to be sure. However, to buy on margin, you must put up an amount equal to the amount you wish to borrow by pledging other cash or securities in your brokerage account. Interest on a margin account moves up or down based on current rates and how much you're borrowing.

If the value of your equity drops 30 percent, your broker will request more cash or marginable securities. If you don't supply them pronto, the broker sells your stock, with proceeds used to pay off a portion of the loan. You'll owe him the remainder, with interest to boot.

Don't mess with a margin account unless you're really serious. Before you break even, your margined stock must go up at least as much as you're paying your broker in interest. And if the stock collapses, buying on margin will make your losses much greater. Keep an eagle eye on your margin account so that you aren't surprised by a margin call. Margin buying significantly increases the effects of quickly rising or falling prices, adding greatly to volatility.

For some protection, you might buy put options, which are the right to sell stock at a certain price. If the margined stock drops, the value of your puts would increase and offset most of the losses on your shares. In addition, you can also use stop orders, whereby your broker enters an order to sell once the stock falls below a specified price. Another means of minimizing margin calls is by borrowing less than the 50 percent maximum on the value of your stocks and investing for the most part in blue-chip stocks that are less volatile.

As stated earlier in this chapter, buying on margin retains tax-deductibility up to the amount of your investment income. In light of the curtailing of many other forms of borrowing, this should make margin purchases even more popular. Just make certain you take the necessary precautions to avert major financial problems in dealing with them.

Of course, any real stock investor must be familiar with the stock tables in the morning newspaper. It's important to keep track of your investments, as well as any potential purchases you might make. The strong readership of the seemingly endless tables in the back of financial sections is evidenced every time a mistake is made or some figure is inadvertently deleted. Hundreds of telephone calls from irate readers will be logged throughout the day at a newspaper whenever such gaffes are made. After all, those numbers represent people's money.

For the New York Stock Exchange and the American Stock Exchange, the nation's two largest, the entries include several columns. The first column gives the high and the low price of the stock for the past 52 weeks. The second column features the name of the stock, which is abbreviated by the various news services in a manner that sometimes tries the patience of the reader. Those abbreviations aren't the stock symbol. More than a few investors must remind themselves that IBM is listed alphabetically not by those three letters, but by its moniker as International Business Machines. Listed along with common stocks are warrants, which are designated as "wt." A warrant is the right to buy a certain number of shares of the stock at a specified price until an expiration date. These are often included with the issue of new stock in order to make the deal more attractive. Also listed are preferred stock, designated as "pf." The owners of preferred stock are entitled to a specified payment before any payment can be made to common stock owners, although dividends on preferred stock are not a legal obligation for the firm.

In the third column are the dividends that the stock pays. The fourth column features the yield, which is the annual dividend divided by the stock's closing price presented as a percentage. The size of the dividend is based more on a company's dividend policy than any relative quality of the stock. For example, utilities tend to pay high dividends, while growth companies plow their money back into the company and pay low dividends. In the fifth column is the price-earnings (P-E) ratio for the stock, the result of the closing price of the stock divided by the firm's earnings per share over the past 12 months. A high P-E ratio indicates that investors have high regard for the stock's earnings and growth potential.

In the sixth column are the sales, or number of shares traded, divided by 100. In the next column are the "high," or highest price at which the stock was traded that day, and the "low," or lowest price. The final two columns include the "close," or last price at which the stock changed hands that day, and the "change," or difference in the closing price from the prior day.

Those publicly-held firms that don't meet size and other requirements of the biggest exchanges, or simply don't want to be listed on those exchanges, are traded "over the counter" through a broker member network of the National Association of Securities Dealers. Information on such stocks listed in the newspapers is slightly different. The first column includes the high and low range for the past 52 weeks. The following column includes the name of the stock and dividend. Next come the high, low and last price of the stock, followed by the net change for the day. Note that OTC stocks tend to be more volatile, less known and not as liquid because fewer shares change hands daily.

Trading records of another 1,000 or so stocks are included in many newspapers under the heading "additional bid and asked quotations," and these abbreviated listings include only the highest bid and the closest sale offer.

While reading the stock listings is important to an investor and should be done several times a week, if you find yourself furtively searching for your stocks daily and basing your day's attitude upon the results, stock investing may not be for you. A stock investor must be willing to roll with the punches a bit and accept the good with the bad in hopes of long-term gain. One day's movement in a stock may often be indicative of very little other than a general trend in the market that day.

As discussed in the chapter on hottest investments, the new issues market is booming and many big-name brokerage firms are underwriting the deals on the stocks of these fledgling companies. But the significant portion of the new issues market involves what is known as the "penny stock." These lagged well behind the larger-company stocks during the market rise of the early 1980s. They have provided some investors with surprising returns in recent days, a great many others with big losses. Penny stocks, ranging in price from one cent to $5, have high mortality rates and should be viewed only as a highly speculative portion of one's investment portfolio. Penny issues are stocks of little-known companies traded primarily by brokerage houses based in Denver and Salt Lake City.

"I really got into penny stocks, clipping small items out of newspapers and magazines about up-and-coming ideas and firms, and invested about $2,000, which I saw go to $3,000 and then come down to $700," said Jim, a medical student who dabbled in the penny stock market. "Now I've got a wife and a baby daughter, and I'm going into blue-chip stocks instead. Would I ever buy another penny stock? Never— maybe."

You're simply gambling if you expect the new issue you select will be the next MCI Corp. or Tandy Corp., two former penny stocks that went on to the big time. Yet, when taken somewhat less than seriously, bargain-basement stocks provide speculative plays for investors who frequently take an initial fling with $500 to $2,000 which they are ready, willing and able to lose. Brokers that specialize in penny stocks tend to be aggressive, in some cases making "blind" telephone calls to investors to tout the potential of impressive-sounding new issues. Technology-oriented stocks or "one-idea" companies are typical penny stocks. Most conventional brokers shy away from these high-risk issues, but discount brokerages will execute the orders. Investors frequently follow these stocks through several penny stock investment periodicals. It is not unusual for a penny stock to rise for several months after it is issued based on its good idea, then come crashing down once it becomes evident the company has no real way to put that idea into practice.

The Securities and Exchange Commission urges investors to carefully read prospectuses of any stocks being considered for purchase. Always ask the company in question for its 10-K report made to the SEC, which includes basic financial position devoid of the hype common to annual reports. If you do buy penny stocks, you're probably better off buying several different stocks in the hope that one will hit it big. The penny stock speculator faces higher brokerage commissions because of the low price and large number of shares purchased, and his shares are not as liquid as those of better-known firms. To a great degree, the prospective buyer must depend upon the honesty of the broker touting the stock. Penny stocks have a bad image not only because the management of many of the small companies fail miserably, but because a number of underwriters of new issues and brokers have, quite frankly, turned out to be crooks.

Make no mistake. Investing in penny stocks exits the normal channels of stock market risk and enters the area of crapshoot. You can make money. But you're more likely to lose money.

11 Pick a Planner

It happens in a flash. One morning you wake up and find your neighborhood stockbroker calling himself a financial consultant. Right off, he's trying to sell you a whole range of products, including new-fangled loans for buying a home or expanding your small business. Sounds good. So, you're signing papers left and right, really getting into the idea of spending more time conferring with this guy about your finances, when suddenly the thought occurs to you: "Who asked for this, anyway?"

Or, you see an ad in the newspaper for a financial planner. After he goes over your finances, he points out a real need for more life insurance. Oh, by the way, he also happens to sell life insurance. You wonder: "So what exactly is a financial planner?"

The new tax laws are here and so is the onslaught of the financial planners.

I once attended a conference of financial planners meeting to discuss the problem of the hazy image that the planning profession seems to conjure up in the public's mind. During a break, a fellow with the most enormous gold cuff links I have ever seen sauntered up. He looked like a model for a "Can men wear jewelry?" ad campaign, with enough enormous rings on his fingers to appear as though he'd won a half-dozen Super Bowls. "How can a group of planners this big be so dumb as to overlook race horses as an important investment?" he asked. "The average investor doesn't know what he's missing out on. Thank God I'm around to tell them."

Welcome to the latest stage in the metamorphosis of services offered America's investors. Whether using a designation given by a company, or a lettered degree from a professional college, more than a quarter-million people are calling themselves financial planners these days. Some don't know much at all about doing any plans for anyone. They just know about selling financial products. And another who holds a certificate in planning isn't necessarily any better than someone who doesn't.

Of course, a planner isn't worth much unless you're candid with him, willing to consider advice and able to aim toward goals. One financial planner expressed surprise when, upon asking a young couple what the goal was in setting up a family financial plan, the husband replied: "Why, new furniture for the dining room."

There are obvious reasons why investment companies like the title of planner on their employee nameplates. Billing yourself as someone capable of going over a person's entire financial needs can mean selling a broader range of products. "A big part of our doing all this, expanding into all these areas, is to build a buffer for our business from the obvious volatility of the stock market," said John L. "Launie" Steffens, who as president of Merrill Lynch Consumer Markets is a rising star on Wall Street and architect of many recent changes. "We want each of our brokers to be able to handle 60 to 70 percent of a person's financial problems, to basically become what a general practitioner is in the medical profession."

Other firms also have been expanding out of stock and bond sales. They're wary of a stock market capable of double-digit drops and of clients who leave in droves whenever the bull market turns bear. It's just that Merrill Lynch, biggest of the brokers and most consumer-oriented, always does things in a big way. Its "general practitioners" of finance, for example, receive much of their training in financial planning and insurance from the television screens of Merrill Lynch's new satellite broadcast system.

Is all this hoopla a bit too much too soon? "The only flak we've received thus far, which is probably deserved, is that not all 11,000 of our people calling themselves financial consultants should be carrying that title," said the 45-year-old Steffens as he leaned back in his chair in the plush office at Merrill Lynch headquarters. "Take a guy who's been out there 20 years selling equities. We're really changing how he does business, from selling products to gathering assets."

There are greater financial incentives for brokers—I mean financial consultants—to handle the new offerings. To lessen chances of a client being advised by someone with whom he doesn't see eye to eye, there's a screening program to set up initial meetings with several brokers. These days, insurance offerings are undergoing more "stringent review" in light of the disaster resulting from sales of annuities of Baldwin-United, which went bankrupt. Small businesses are feeling the onslaught of Wall Street, with more credit-line, insurance and pension management packages offered. Brokerage firms seek business that banks, accountants and lawyers traditionally have received. Their first pitches have been made to businessmen who have personal investment accounts with the firm.

There's new emphasis on the margin account, traditionally used to buy securities, for general purpose loans. It's based on securities previously considered non-marginable, such as certificates of deposit held with the brokerage firm. Loan charge is 8 to 10 percent, depending on its size. "Our Flexible Credit Account can be used for either business purposes or other investments, such as real estate," said an executive with Merrill Lynch Credit Management Group. "Minimum loan is $25,000, and the loan is open, a concept that makes it possible to consider credit management in the same way as your investment management."

Be aware. Wall Street firms want entry into every part of an investor's financial dealings. The investor must assess the quality of each service offered, because no financial institution has been able to do all things equally well.

The concept of financial guidance these days extends far beyond Wall Street, however.

Financial planners seem to be everywhere, their conferences and seminars proliferating as a truly modern phenomenon. In the course of my covering the investment community, I've received hundreds of business cards and press releases from planners seeking the limelight. Most are pleasant enough, some with a bit of the salesman in their personality, a few pushing investments that have turned out to be less than successful for their clients (as in the case of some troubled energy partnerships).

More Americans are seeking out financial planners to guide them along a path to economic security. It's wise to get a professional opinion about your money. Yet most investors have little concept of what a financial planner is, what sort of services should be expected and how much the full treatment might cost. Even the expanding financial planner "industry" is a bit mixed up on those points. "A financial planner should be someone who can analyze a family's total needs in areas such as investment, taxes, insurance, educational goals and retirement, and put it all together in a plan," said Hubert L. Harris, executive director of the 21,000-member International Association for Financial Planning, based in Atlanta.

Some planners are brokers, or accountants, or lawyers, or insurance agents, or bankers, who may be perfectly competent but have no formal planner designations. Still others are one-product sales people who have never prepared a financial plan. "Many people calling themselves financial planners don't have an inkling about planning, calculating net worth, analyzing cash flow or devising budgets," said Marvin W. Tuttle, a spokesman for the Institute of Certified Financial Planners, an 18,000-member trade group based in Denver.

Some form of regulation of this growing field is likely in the near future, perhaps at the federal level. The Denver group is pushing for a system of self-regulation, while the rival Atlanta group favors direct government regulation, preferably at the state level using standard guidelines. (Some planners are covered by other regulations, as in the case of attorneys or brokers.) Whatever regulations may come to pass, keep these basics in mind if you're shopping for a planner today:

—There are a number of professional designations. The "certified financial planner" designation is given by the Denver group on completion of a self-study course and examination. Thus far, there are about 10,000 graduates. In addition, American College in Bryn Mawr, Pa., grants a "chartered financial consultant" designation. And, of course, some investment firms give financial consultant designations to staffers who have completed company-sponsored courses of study.

—Fees for a financial plan vary widely, costing from several hundred dollars to several thousand. Though it may be possible to receive a $50 computer plan as a starting point, it is not unusual to spend a large sum if a client has high net worth or a complicated situation. In some cases, the fee is based upon a percentage of the client's net worth. Some planners require an up-front fee. In all cases, find out all fees in advance, so that you won't be socked with unexpected costs later. For example, some planners may charge $100 an hour when work goes beyond a certain duration. Use your initial visit to get acquainted with the planner, to see whether your personalities and goals match up and to get an estimate of what a plan would cost. If you do become a client, expect a written plan that clearly states objectives and goals and gives specific recommendations for attaining them.

A financial plan should be easy to understand and have clear recommendations. It must include your income and net worth. It should take a close look at your investment portfolio, insurance coverage, loans and taxes. There should be a realistic game plan for meeting your goals. Of course, no one says you have to follow the suggestions or agree with the plan. You've paid your money for suggestions, not a binding contract. Keep in mind that, during the forming of the plan, you'll likely have to provide important financial data about your family. You should be candid in discussing problem areas so that the planner is dealing with accurate information. There should also be periodic review with the planner, to take into account your progress or changing circumstances.

"There was nothing really dramatic that came from our plan, although it did get us to think realistically for the first time about putting money aside for retirement," a woman in her mid-50s told me after she and her husband had gone over a plan put together for them which included an inheritance recently received. "It helps to have an unbiased person look over what you're doing, particularly if that person has some ideas for getting higher yields on your money."

—Shop around before selecting a planner. Use the same process you would to select a family doctor, considering recommendations of friends and credentials of the planner. You can get names of planners in your area from the International Association for Financial Planning, Two Concourse Parkway, Suite 800, Atlanta, Ga. 30328; Institute of Certified Financial Planners, 10065 E. Harvard Ave., Denver, Colo. 80231; the International Association of Registered Financial Planners, 4127 W. Cypress St., Tampa, Fla. 33607; and the American Society of CLU, 270 Bryn Mawr Ave., Bryn Mawr, Pa. 19010. Be wary of anyone who throws around the word "wealth" too often or seems busier with spouting inflated promises than going over the nuts-and-bolts of a valid plan.

—Many planners sell financial products. They should explain this up-front, so that you can determine whether these specific products have a bearing on the plan suggested for you. Most sales people wind up with a commission of 1 to 10 percent for the products they sell. Always find out the commission before you pay, since it can definitely affect what your total yield will be on your money.

—Many planners are registered as investment advisers with the Securities and Exchange Commission. While such registration makes public the planner's background, products he sells and his fee schedule, remember that it does not really pass judgment on the professional competence of the planner.

Whether you decide to go with a planner with a brokerage firm, some other type of financial institution or an independent planner, there's a good chance you're likely to be advised to consolidate your financial holdings into one type of account or a related group of accounts. This streamlining of financial services is a part of the overall modern services plan that investment companies are pushing.

The various "all-in-one" investment accounts that draw your financial holdings together in a streamlined package can be a great idea—as long as you're not just opening one to keep up with the Joneses. Spawned nearly a decade ago, these central assets accounts are offered under many different names by brokerage firms, banks and insurance companies.

They typically include a brokerage and checking account, margin account, mutual funds and credit or debit card. A handy monthly statement details your investments and transactions, and dividends are regularly swept into a money market account so you earn interest as quickly as possible. A raft of additional features are offered by various competitors, such as automated teller machines, telephone bill-paying, traveler's checks or direct deposit of paychecks. The minimum investment usually ranges from $10,000 to $20,000, with annual fees ranging from $25 to $100. Unless you're convinced you'll really use many of those features, that substantial commitment may not be justified.

Keep in mind that a broker handling such an account will likely use that neatly compiled data about your personal finances as a blueprint to sell you still more investments. These streamlined accounts definitely lend themselves to overall handling by an investment professional. Promoting its Cash Management Account as the "real badge of affluence," Merrill Lynch remains the industry leader with $85 billion in assets. Acknowledging that not everyone can afford the $20,000 minimum and $65 annual fee, the company recently introduced its Capital Builder Account offering fewer frills, a $5,000 minimum and $40 annual fee.

The Prudential-Bache Command Account, Fidelity Ultra Service Account and Citibank Focus Account are examples of the dozens of competing accounts offering their own idiosyncrasies. "Our Active Assets Account has grown steadily the past several years, though it slowed a bit last year, perhaps because we raised our annual fee to $80," explained an executive at Dean Witter Reynolds. "Features have increased, including a shopping service that permits you to order merchandise by phone." The public often thinks such accounts are exactly alike, and sometimes the firms advertising them don't alter that opinion. A study by the Better Business Bureau of Metropolitan New York cited problems such as inaccurate printed material, failure to provide prospectuses and inconsistent telephone advice.

It's important to compare several central assets accounts. Find out whether the sweep to the money market account is done daily or weekly, and whether it includes all cash or just an amount above a certain level. Find out whether you'll receive canceled checks and what office you contact in case of any mix-up. (Most accounts offer a toll-free number for assistance.) If it includes a debit card rather than a conventional credit card, your charges will be deducted from your account in full each month. Compare sample monthly statements to see which accounts are most helpful. Decide whether you're willing to pay more for some of the fancier optional features. Keep in mind that an account offered through a discount brokerage firm or a bank will offer you less expensive transaction costs than a full-service broker when buying stocks or bonds.

Be cautious, since these large accounts make it easier to

erode important family assets through charges and check-writing if you don't monitor them. It's possible for someone not keeping track to spend too much of his family's capital. Use a central assets account to invest, not overextend.

What's in a plan

Average investors often wonder what a financial plan is all about, but aren't so anxious to open up their financial lives to a stranger. So we've done it for you. Following are two financial plans done up by Shearson Lehman Brothers that take into account the new tax laws and how best to invest under them. It should be noted that Shearson most certainly sells financial products and obviously wants to sell some to those it counsels. Many "fee-only" planners might speak more generally among a variety of investments, or might zero in more on family budgeting than strictly instruments. But these plans do give you an idea of the sort of scrutiny and advice you'd receive. The names given are fictitious and the advice is strictly that of the firm which has done the plan, not this author's.

Personal Review
O · U · T · L · I · N · E

Confidential
PERSONAL REVIEW
for
Jane Clemens

INVESTMENT CONCERNS

Your major investment objective for your personal assets, as we understand it, is to increase your assets. You are 38 and your total annual income is about $41,500. You consider yourself an aggressive investor. We have estimated your net worth, total assets minus total liabilities, to be over $172,000. It is comprised primarily of closely held business interests, your residence and mutual funds.

ASSET REALLOCATION SCHEDULE

In the following schedule, we summarize how your assets are currently allocated and how your portfolio would appear after our recommendations have been implemented. Our recommendations are based on information supplied by you. If your situation has changed, please notify your Financial Consultant, Anthony Morsey, to make the appropriate adjustments. Our recommendations should be regarded as a starting point for discussion in developing the appropriate investment strategies.

Personal Review
O·U·T·L·I·N·E

ASSET REALLOCATION SCHEDULE

Current Assets	Present Position	Recommended Change	Proposed Position
Short-term Municipal Fund	$9,000	($4,000)	$5,000
Checking/Savings	3,000	(3,000)	0
Corporate Bonds	4,800	(4,800)	0
Single Premium Life Insurance	0	5,500	5,500
Municipal Bond Unit Trusts	0	10,000	10,000
Stock Mutual Funds	13,500	(3,700)	9,800
Total Current Assets	$30,300	$0	$30,300

Retirement Assets			
Jane's IRA Accounts:			
Certificates Of Deposit	2,300	0	2,300
Real Estate Income Partnerships	0	2,000	2,000
Next IRA Contribution	2,000	(2,000)	0
Income Fund/Trust	3,800	0	3,800
Jane's Keogh Accounts:			
Certificates Of Deposit	5,000	0	5,000
Real Estate Income Partnerships	2,000	0	2,000
Total Deferred Assets	$15,100	$0	$15,100
Total Assets	$45,400	$0	$45,400

Personal Review
O · U · T · L · I · N · E

Jane Clemens
Page 3

ALLOCATION CHARTS

The charts below illustrate the present and proposed allocation of your portfolio in the areas of Current Assets and Retirement Assets. Retirement Assets include your IRA and Keogh accounts.

A discussion of our recommendations in those areas follows. In addition, we review the areas of Risk Management and Estate Planning as they relate to your financial future.

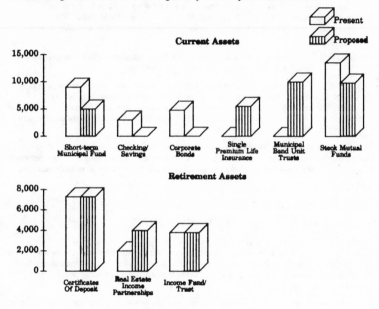

INVESTMENT PLANNING

The objective in developing an investment plan is to build a portfolio of investments that meet several, sometimes conflicting, goals. Only by analyzing your investment objectives and your available resources can you begin to develop a program that meets your needs. This allows you to control your investment strategy and to avoid the all-too-common problem of simply collecting investments because you thought they were a good buy. Each investment must be judged not only on its own merits but also on its position within your portfolio. The investment must enable you to achieve one or more of your financial objectives.

Personal Review

O · U · T · L · I · N · E

We have tailored our recommendations to match your aggressive investment preference. We have also considered your current financial situation and today's economic conditions. In terms of the current economic environment, we believe the following four factors will shape present investment opportunities:

● Interest rates have declined and should remain low since inflation is expected to remain low.

● Real rates of return (nominal rate minus current inflation rate) on fixed income investments are high and should remain at attractive levels for the near future. In conjunction with low interest rates, now is the time to lock in rates available on longer term investments.

● The U.S. dollar should continue to decline. Multinational stocks, global mutual funds, or an international unit trust should offer profit opportunities.

● Finally, stocks have entered a trading range, but selected issues will provide good rates of total return through dividends and appreciation. Increased earnings per share will fuel continued appreciation and foreign investors are purchasing U.S. stocks now that the dollar has corrected. Areas that will benefit from these economic changes include basic industries, capital goods, and technology.

Your Financial Consultant, Anthony Morsey, can discuss the specific impact each of these factors will have on our recommended allocation. In addition, future changes in your personal situation, as well as new tax legislation, will require you to review certain recommendations.

CASH MANAGEMENT

12,000   5,000

The first step in any allocation of investment assets is to establish a cash reserve. This reserve must function as a "working account" from which you can pay current expenses and it must provide a reserve for emergencies. In addition, it should serve as an "opportunity fund" for uncommitted assets and as a temporary "parking place" for funds which will be needed for major expenses in the near future.

As a general rule, your working account should allow you to pay your regular living expenses for the next two to six months. This will depend on the predictability and regularity of your other sources of income, the liquidity of your other assets and your own comfort level. If you establish a reserve at the low end of this range, you should probably add an additional amount for emergencies. Based on the information you have provided, we think a cash reserve of $5,000 will be adequate for your purposes.

For your cash reserve, we suggest using the Muni Fund with your current Financial Management Account. This will provide you with the maximum after-tax income. Due to market conditions, yields on the funds change over time. You should periodically compare the yields on these funds to determine which one is best for you.

In reallocating your portfolio, we have established your cash reserve at a level we feel is consistent with your needs for liquidity on an everyday basis. This will allow you to invest

Personal Review
O · U · T · L · I · N · E

more of your assets in higher yielding investments. We are aware that this cash reserve is less than the amount you currently have set aside in readily available funds such as money market funds and savings.

If you would prefer to keep a larger portion of your funds liquid, you may wish to use municipal bonds with a "put" feature as a secondary source of liquidity. The "put" feature permits you to sell the bonds at par value prior to maturity. This feature stablizes the market value of the bonds, because the risk of loss of principal due to higher interest rates is reduced.

CURRENT ASSETS

Within your current portfolio, you should be looking to achieve a balance between your need for current spendable income and your future needs. Unlike your retirement assets, your current assets are not sheltered from income taxes. When investing these assets for income, it is important to evaluate returns on an after-tax basis.

New tax legislation for 1987 will dramatically alter tax planning for many investors. A more comprehensive definition of taxable income and reduced tax rates will require investors to look ahead to the changes in their own situations. To the extent possible, we have based our recommendations on the provisions of the new law.

Given your effective marginal tax bracket, which we have estimated at 36%, we suggest you concentrate on tax-exempt issues. You would need to earn 10.4% on a taxable investment to equal the 7.5% return available on high quality, long-term municipal issues. Our estimate is based on the changes in tax rates that will become fully effective in March 1987. Your effective marginal tax bracket represents how much of an additional dollar of taxable investment income will be paid in federal and state income taxes. For example, when you receive $100 in interest, you must pay $36 in federal and state income taxes. In computing this rate, we have taken into account the deductibility of state taxes on your federal tax return.

To add balance and diversity to your portfolio, we suggest you commit a portion of your current assets for growth. Such a strategy will provide you with the potential to increase your assets at a rate significantly above the inflation rate. Your ability to accumulate assets before your retirement will be an important element in determining your lifestyle after you stop working.

Municipal Unit Trust

0   10,000

As a way to earn tax-free income, we suggest you invest $10,000 in a municipal unit trust. Unit trusts represent a way to participate in a selected portfolio of bonds. The securities initially selected remain in the trust throughout its life and do not change. The yield on a unit trust is fixed, based on your purchase price. Income is paid monthly, and can be re-invested in additional units of the trust, if you wish. Since adding to your current cash flow is not your major objective, we suggest you re-invest your monthly income in additional shares of the unit

Personal Review
O · U · T · L · I · N · E

trust.

You can choose from a variety of municipal unit trusts. In addition to short-term, intermediate, and long-term series, there is a "floating rate" series where the interest rate fluctuates with general interest rates so that the principal value is protected. The "insured" series is comprised of bonds that are guaranteed to pay interest and principal when they are due. Finally, since you are a Massachusetts State resident, you may wish to review the yield from the unit trust composed entirely of Massachusetts bonds. The income from this series will be exempt from local, Massachusetts state and federal income taxes.

Single Premium Life Investment Plan

0   5,500

We suggest you commit $5,500 to a single premium life investment plan. This new insurance product offers you the benefits of several different investments: the tax deferral available from an annuity, the tax-free cash flow of a municipal bond, the options and growth potential of mutual funds, and the benefits of life insurance.

You have a choice of investing your funds in either a fixed interest contract or in a variable contract with several mutual fund alternatives. As with an annuity, increases in your cash value are free of current income taxes. These increases can also be borrowed on a tax-free basis; repayment is not required and the loan is made at very low rates. Finally, because this investment is a life insurance policy, your beneficiaries will receive an income tax-free death benefit in excess of the policy's cash value.

You retain these advantages as long as your single premium life investment plan remains in force. Should you surrender your policy, all earnings will be subject to income taxes, so this investment should be viewed on a long-term basis.

Corporate Bonds

4,800   0

Your new portfolio reflects the elimination of your corporate bonds. This change is not a reflection on the quality of any individual bond. Rather, we feel that your portfolio should be adjusted to better meet your needs. However, before you implement this strategy, we suggest you review your holdings more closely with your Financial Consultant. The new tax law makes this review very timely due to the changes in capital gains rates.

Business Interests

Your business is valued at $100,000. As you know, there are a number of tax benefits available to a business owner, especially in the retirement plan area. Also, certain investments, such as money market preferred stock, have been recently introduced to meet the special needs and tax situation of a corporation. Your Financial Consultant can review your situation more thoroughly to allow you to take maximum advantage of your business.

Personal Review
O · U · T · L · I · N · E

RETIREMENT ASSETS

Your personal retirement assets are valued at $15,100. To capture the high yields currently available, we suggest that you concentrate on income-oriented vehicles.

Real Estate Income Partnerships

2,000 4,000

We recommend that you add $2,000 to your holdings of income partnerships. These investments offer a high current yield and the potential for capital appreciation. Specially-designed partnerships provide the opportunity to participate in a diversified portfolio consisting primarily of wrap-around mortgage loans with an equity participation. You receive quarterly cash distributions from cash flow plus additional cash distributions from deferred interest. Finally, there is the potential to profit from an increase in the value of the real estate when the property is sold.

IRA Contribution

As part of our analysis, we have shown our investment recommendations for your next IRA contribution. If you have not made a contribution based on your earnings for this year, we suggest you do so as soon as feasible. If you have already made your contribution, we recommend you contribute to your IRA early next year so as to earn the maximum income on your investment.

In your situation, $2,000 is the maximum contribution.

Contributions to an IRA for 1986 are tax-deductible and all the earnings within the plan are tax-deferred until they are withdrawn. Upon withdrawal, all the funds are taxed as ordinary income. Should you make a withdrawal before age 59½, you will also be subject to a penalty tax equal to 10% of the distribution.

As you are probably aware, beginning in 1987, if you are covered by a corporate retirement plan, the full tax deduction for IRA contribution will only be available if your adjusted gross income is below $25,000. You would be entitled to a partial deduction if your income is between $25,000 and $35,000. No deduction is allowed if your income is above this limit. Contributions would remain fully deductible, regardless of your income, if you are not covered by a company retirement plan.

The new law only involves the deductibility of IRA contributions. All workers, regardless of income or pension coverage, would be allowed to contribute to an IRA, where earnings will continue to be tax-deferred. Since there is a penalty for withdrawals prior to age 59½, it is important that you view the program as a long-term strategy. Although the current tax advantage of an IRA contribution may be reduced for you, we feel the flexibility and tax-deferral available with this investment will be a critical element in meeting your retirement goals.

To illustrate the effect of annual IRA contributions, should you continue to invest $2,000 in an IRA for the next 27 years, your account would be worth $267,400 if it grew at 9% annually.

Personal Review

O · U · T · L · I · N · E

RETIREMENT PLANNING

Keogh Retirement Plan

Since you have self-employment income, you can contribute to a Keogh Plan as a way to reduce taxes and provide funds for retirement. As you know, the contribution is limited to the lesser of $30,000 or 20% of net profit reported on Schedule C. Contributions can be made to the account up until the time to file the tax return, including extensions.

RISK MANAGEMENT

Although we have discussed investment planning first, we want to emphasize the importance of allocating enough of your resources, before making investment decisions, to provide adequate insurance coverage. This includes making provision for funds in the event of your death or disability as well as protecting your assets. Accordingly, we recommend a review of your life, disability and liability insurance coverages.

Life Insurance

Many single people, such as yourself, do not carry any life insurance coverage. If you feel your current assets are sufficient to cover your estate settlement costs, such as legal fees, loan repayments, and estate taxes, we agree with your decision. You may wish to review your situation though due to the recent introduction of a new concept in insurance coverage, known as Universal Life. Unlike traditional life insurance, Universal Life is also an attractive investment vehicle. It has the low cost associated with term insurance and the cash value build-up associated with permanent insurance, including a high current interest rate. The earnings in the policy are tax-deferred and can be borrowed out to provide a ready source of cash when needed. You can alter the amount of insurance coverage on a continuing basis as your financial situation changes.

Another alternative is the purchase of a Single Premium Life Investment Plan that was recommended earlier in this report. Both types of policies offer you an attractive investment vehicle with insurance coverage.

Your Financial Consultant can provide you a no-cost service to help you more precisely determine your insurance needs to meet your financial objectives.

Disability Income

If you have not done so recently, we suggest that you review the disability income protection available from your employer. Your future earning power is an asset worthy of protection.

Generally speaking, your coverage should provide you with benefits equal to about two-thirds of your pre-tax earnings. If additional protection is needed, you can purchase an individual policy. Disability income benefits from a policy you own are paid to you as tax-free income, should you ever need to collect them. A wide variety of coverages are available. Your Financial Consultant, Anthony Morsey, can assist you in making the appropriate selection.

Personal Review
O · U · T · L · I · N · E

Homeowner's and Liability Insurance

A periodic review of your homeowner's policy is a worthwhile investment of your time. We recommend that the policy limits on your insurance cover at least 80 percent of your home's current replacement cost. If you bought the policy several years ago, the increase in the value of your home may place your coverage below this limit. In that event, you should have it reviewed in order to assure maximum recovery in the event of a partial loss.

If you do not already own an umbrella liability policy, we suggest you consider purchasing such a policy. This type of policy both increases the dollar amount of your protection and covers additional hazards. The policy operates over and above your underlying liability insurance.

At a minimum, we suggest you consider a policy for $1,000,000. Although this will provide you substantially higher protection, the annual premium is modest (e.g., $150-$200 per year). We feel it is a worthwhile investment to provide peace of mind and to insulate your assets from a large liability claim.

ESTATE PLANNING

Since you are single, you may not feel it is necessary to have a will. There are disadvantages, even for a single person, if a will is not executed. In general, your assets will be distributed according to Massachusetts state law, which may not coincide with your own wishes. Also, without a will, the court will appoint an administrator, not your own selected executor, who will oversee your estate. Therefore, although there may not be any tax savings with a will, we feel there are significant non-tax advantages to having a will. We suggest you consult with your attorney regarding the execution of a will.

Personal Review
O · U · T · L · I · N · E

SUMMARY

The charts below summarize how your assets are presently allocated and how your portfolio would change after our recommendations have been implemented. We have tried to structure your assets to meet your goals and objectives based on your current situation. Achieving your financial objectives is an ongoing process that needs to be closely monitored and adjusted to changing conditions. Your Financial Consultant, Anthony Morsey, can help design an investment strategy that is appropriate for your needs.

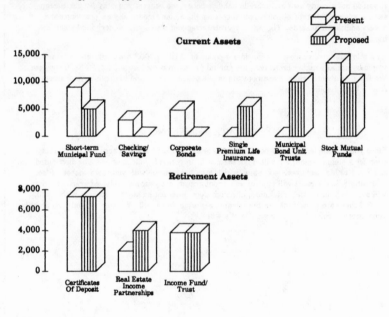

Personal Review
O · U · T · L · I · N · E

Confidential
PERSONAL REVIEW
for
Sam and Janet Evening

INVESTMENT CONCERNS

Your major investment objective for your personal assets, as we understand it, is to increase your assets. Your ages are 36 and 35 and your total annual income is about $65,000. You consider yourself a moderate investor. We have estimated your net worth, total assets minus total liabilities, to be over $145,000. It is comprised primarily of your residence, retirement plans and money market funds.

ASSET REALLOCATION SCHEDULE

In the following schedule, we summarize how your assets are currently allocated and how your portfolio would appear after our recommendations have been implemented.

Personal Review
O · U · T · L · I · N · E

Sam and Janet Evening
Page 2

ASSET REALLOCATION SCHEDULE

Current Assets	Present Position	Recommended Change	Proposed Position
Cash Value Of Whole Life Insurance	$4,500	($4,500)	$0
Short-term Municipal Fund	0	6,000	6,000
Taxable Money Market Fund	4,000	(4,000)	0
Checking/Savings	2,000	(2,000)	0
Tax-Free Money Market Fund	2,000	(2,000)	0
Municipal Bond Mutual Funds	5,800	6,500	12,300
Common Stocks	4,500	0	4,500
Total Current Assets	$22,800	$0	$22,800

Retirement Assets

	Present Position	Recommended Change	Proposed Position
Sam's IRA Accounts:			
Certificates Of Deposit	4,000	0	4,000
Next IRA Contribution	2,000	(2,000)	0
Income Fund/Trust	0	2,000	2,000
Stocks	1,800	0	1,800
Zero Coupon Bonds	1,200	0	1,200
Janet's IRA Accounts:			
Money Market Funds	3,000	(3,000)	0
Real Estate Income Partnerships	0	4,000	4,000
Next IRA Contribution	2,000	(2,000)	0
Income Fund/Trust	0	4,500	4,500
Zero Coupon Bonds	2,000	(2,000)	0
Growth Fund/Trust	1,500	(1,500)	0
Total Deferred Assets	$17,500	$0	$17,500
Total Assets	$40,300	$0	$40,300

Personal Review

O · U · T · L · I · N · E

Sam and Janet Evening
Page 3

ALLOCATION CHARTS

The charts below illustrate the present and proposed allocation of your portfolio in the areas of Current Assets and Retirement Assets. Retirement Assets include your IRA accounts.

A discussion of our recommendations in those areas follows. In addition, we review the areas of Risk Management, Estate Planning and Liability Management as they relate to your financial future.

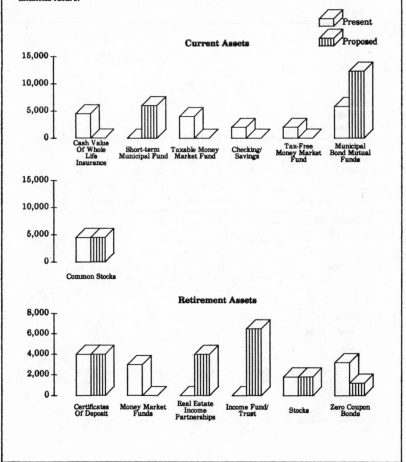

Personal Review

O · U · T · L · I · N · E

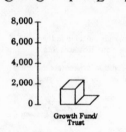

8,000
6,000
4,000
2,000
0

Growth Fund/
Trust

INVESTMENT PLANNING

The objective in developing an investment plan is to build a portfolio of investments that meet several, sometimes conflicting, goals. Only by analyzing your investment objectives and your available resources can you begin to develop a program that meets your needs. This allows you to control your investment strategy and to avoid the all-too-common problem of simply collecting investments because you thought they were a good buy. Each investment must be judged not only on its own merits but also on its position within your portfolio. The investment must enable you to achieve one or more of your financial objectives.

We have tailored our recommendations to match your moderate investment preference. We have also considered your current financial situation and today's economic conditions. In terms of the current economic environment, we believe the following four factors will shape present investment opportunities:

● Interest rates have declined and should remain low since inflation is expected to remain low.

● Real rates of return (nominal rate minus current inflation rate) on fixed income investments are high and should remain at attractive levels for the near future. In conjunction with low interest rates, now is the time to lock in rates available on longer term investments.

● The U.S. dollar should continue to decline. Multinational stocks, global mutual funds, or an international unit trust should offer profit opportunities.

● Finally, stocks have entered a trading range, but selected issues will provide good rates of total return through dividends and appreciation. Increased earnings per share will fuel continued appreciation and foreign investors are purchasing U.S. stocks now that the dollar has corrected. Areas that will benefit from these economic changes include basic industries, capital goods, and technology.

Your Financial Consultant can discuss the specific impact each of these factors will have on our recommended allocation. In addition, future changes in your personal situation, as well as new tax legislation, will require you to review certain recommendations.

Personal Review
O·U·T·L·I·N·E

8,000 6,000

CASH MANAGEMENT

The first step in any allocation of investment assets is to establish a cash reserve. This reserve must function as a "working account" from which you can pay current expenses and it must provide a reserve for emergencies. In addition, it should serve as an "opportunity fund" for uncommitted assets and as a temporary "parking place" for funds which will be needed for major expenses in the near future.

As a general rule, your working account should allow you to pay your regular living expenses for the next two to six months. This will depend on the predictability and regularity of your other sources of income, the liquidity of your other assets and your own comfort level. If you establish a reserve at the low end of this range, you should probably add an additional amount for emergencies. Based on the information you have provided, we think a cash reserve of $6,000 will be adequate for your purposes.

The Financial Management Account (FMA) is an ideal place for your cash reserve. It combines a money market account, checking account, brokerage account, and an American Express Gold Card. Combining these elements into one account provides you a powerful tool for managing your financial affairs.

For your cash reserve, we suggest using the Muni Fund available with the Financial Management Account. This will provide you with the maximum after-tax income. Due to market conditions, yields on the funds change over time. You should periodically compare the yields on these funds to determine which one is best for you.

CURRENT ASSETS

Within your current portfolio, you should be looking to achieve a balance between your need for current spendable income and your future needs. Unlike your retirement assets, your current assets are not sheltered from income taxes. When investing these assets for income, it is important to evaluate returns on an after-tax basis.

New tax legislation for 1987 will dramatically alter tax planning for many investors. A more comprehensive definition of taxable income and reduced tax rates will require investors to look ahead to the changes in their own situations. To the extent possible, we have based our recommendations on the provisions of the new law.

Given your effective marginal tax bracket, which we have estimated at 36%, we suggest you concentrate on tax-exempt issues. You would need to earn 10.4% on a taxable investment to equal the 7.5% return available on high quality, long-term municipal issues. Our estimate is based on the changes in tax rates that will become fully effective in March 1987. Your effective marginal tax bracket represents how much of an additional dollar of taxable investment income will be paid in federal and state income taxes. For example, when you receive $100 in interest, you must pay $36 in federal and state income taxes. In computing

Personal Review
O · U · T · L · I · N · E

this rate, we have taken into account the deductibility of state taxes on your federal tax return.

To add balance and diversity to your portfolio, we suggest you commit a portion of your current assets for growth. Such a strategy will provide you with the potential to increase your assets at a rate significantly above the inflation rate. Your ability to accumulate assets before your retirement will be an important element in determining your lifestyle after you stop working.

Municipal Bond Mutual Funds

5,800 12,300

For your needs, a municipal bond mutual fund is an excellent way to provide tax-free income. This kind of fund invests in a diversified portfolio of municipal bonds with different issuers and maturity dates. The fund is managed on a day-to-day basis for optimal performance. By utilizing a fund that is a member of a family of funds, you have exchange privileges with other members of the group. Income is paid monthly. If you wish, the earnings can be re-invested to compound on a tax-free basis. We suggest an investment of $6,500 bringing your holdings to $12,300.

RETIREMENT ASSETS

Your personal retirement assets are valued at $17,500. To meet your objectives, we feel that your retirement assets should be divided between income and growth vehicles. The income investments will allow you to capture the high yields currently available on a tax-deferred basis. The growth vehicles will provide you the opportunity to increase your assets for retirement.

Income Funds / Unit Trusts

0 6,500

One way to invest for a high yield is through the use of an income mutual fund or unit trust. We suggest an investment of $6,500. Both mutual funds and unit trusts allow you to invest in a diversified portfolio of issuers.

Since the securities selected for a unit trust remain in the trust until they mature or are redeemed, the yield from the investment is fixed. Thus, when interest rates are declining, they are an attractive vehicle. Mutual funds are managed on a more active basis. The success of income mutual funds is influenced by interest rate moves in general and the skill of the fund manager.

Personal Review
O · U · T · L · I · N · E

Real Estate Income Partnerships

0   4,000

A real estate partnership designed especially for tax-deferred accounts is an attractive investment for you. We think an investment of $4,000 would be a wise use of your funds. These partnerships are designed to offer a high current yield with capital appreciation potential. They provide you with the opportunity to participate in a diversified portfolio consisting primarily of wrap-around mortgage loans with an equity participation. You receive quarterly cash distributions from cash flow, plus additional cash distributions from deferred interest and the potential to profit from an increase in the value of real estate when the property is sold.

Money Market Funds

3,000   0

We have eliminated your money market funds and used the proceeds in redesigning your portfolio. Given the current yield on money market funds, we feel you can improve your return by considering some of the investments discussed earlier.

IRA Contribution

As part of our analysis, we have shown our investment recommendations for your next IRA contribution. If you have not made a contribution based on your earnings for this year, we suggest you do so as soon as feasible. Since you both work, you can make a maximum contribution of $4,000.

Contributions to an IRA are tax-deductible and all the earnings within the plan are tax-deferred until they are withdrawn. Upon withdrawal, all the funds are taxed as ordinary income. Should you make a withdrawal before age 59½, you will also be subject to a penalty tax equal to 10% of the distribution.

As you are probably aware, beginning in 1987, if you are covered by a corporate retirement plan, the full tax deduction for IRA contribution will only be available if your adjusted gross income is below $40,000. Couples with income between $40,000 and $50,000 would be entitled to a partial deduction. Deductions would be disallowed for incomes above this limit. The rules apply if either spouse is covered by a retirement plan. Contributions would remain fully deductible, regardless of your income, if neither of you is covered by a company retirement plan.

The new law only involves the deductibility of IRA contributions. All workers, regardless of income or pension coverage, would be allowed to contribute to an IRA, where earnings will continue to be tax-deferred. Since there is a penalty for withdrawals prior to age 59½, it is important that you view the program as a long-term strategy. Although the current tax advantage of an IRA contribution may be reduced for you, we feel the flexibility and tax-deferral available with this investment will be a critical element in meeting your retirement

goals.

To illustrate the effect of annual IRA contributions, should you continue to invest $2,000 in an IRA for the next 29 years, your account would be worth $333,400 if it grew at 9% annually. Over a period of 30 years Janet's IRA would grow to $358,800.

EDUCATION FUNDING

You have indicated an interest in providing education funding for a child. The new tax has dramatically altered some of the income shifting techniques used in the past. Beginning in 1987, for children under the age of 14, unearned income of more than $1,000 will be taxed at your marginal tax bracket. This applies to custodial accounts established under the Uniform Gifts to Minor Act (UGMA) or the Uniform Transfers to Minor Act (UTMA). These rules apply regardless of when the account was established. The rules also apply to Clifford and spousal remainder trusts created after March 1, 1986.

These new rules have important implications in building a college education fund in the most tax effective way. For example, if there are unrealized capital gains in a child's account, you may wish to recognize the gains this year to take advantage of the child's lower tax bracket. For a child under the age of 14 with assets that produce more than $1,000 of income annually, you may wish to shift a portion of the child's assets to tax advantaged investments such as municipal bonds, annuities or a single premium life investment. Your financial Consultant can structure a portfolio to take advantage of the child's tax situation.

Special Services

From the information you provided, it appears you could benefit from a specific analysis in the areas of:

- income tax projections.

- credit management opportunities.

- insurance planning.

- professional money manager services.

- trust management.

That type of analysis is beyond the scope of this report since more specific and detailed information is needed. We suggest you discuss your situation with your Financial Consultant who has a number of services and programs designed to meet your needs.

Personal Review
O · U · T · L · I · N · E

RISK MANAGEMENT

Although we have discussed investment planning first, we want to emphasize the importance of allocating enough of your resources, before making investment decisions, to provide adequate insurance coverage. This includes making provision for funds in the event of your death or disability as well as protecting your assets. Accordingly, we recommend a review of your life, disability and liability insurance coverages.

Life Insurance

You should consider the income needs of your family in the event of your death. Those needs would be met through earnings on the combination of your liquid investment assets and life insurance proceeds. Your current investable assets of $18,300 plus current life insurance coverage of $250,000 would provide an annual income of about $21,500 if invested at an after-tax yield of eight percent. In addition, Janet may be entitled to Social Security benefits, but not until she reaches age 60. This amount should be compared to the income required to maintain your family's current standard of living. The effects of future inflation should also be considered in your analysis.

If additional survivor income is necessary, the purchase of a Universal Life insurance policy should be considered. This type of insurance has the low cost associated with term insurance and the cash value build-up associated with permanent insurance, including a high current interest rate. You can alter the amount of insurance coverage on a continuing basis as your financial situation changes.

Your Financial Consultant can provide you a no-cost service to more precisely determine the amount of insurance needed to meet your financial objectives. An evaluation of your present insurance policies is part of this free service. This will allow you to determine whether your current coverage is competitive with some of the newer products available such as Universal Life.

Disability Income

If you have not done so recently, we suggest that you review the disability income protection available from your employer. Your future earning power is an asset worthy of protection.

Generally speaking, your coverage should provide you with benefits equal to about two-thirds of your pre-tax earnings. If additional protection is needed, you can purchase an individual policy. Disability income benefits from a policy you own are paid to you as tax-free income, should you ever need to collect them. A wide variety of coverages are available. Your Financial Consultant, Doug Kalish, can assist you in making the appropriate selection.

Homeowner's and Liability Insurance

A periodic review of your homeowner's policy is a worthwhile investment of your time. We recommend that the policy limits on your insurance cover at least 80 percent of your home's current replacement cost. If you bought the policy several years ago, the increase in the value of your home may place your coverage below this limit. In that event, you should have it reviewed in order to assure maximum recovery in the event of a partial loss.

Personal Review
O · U · T · L · I · N · E

If you do not already own an umbrella liability policy, we suggest you consider purchasing such a policy. This type of policy both increases the dollar amount of your protection and covers additional hazards. The policy operates over and above your underlying liability insurance.

At a minimum, we suggest you consider a policy for $1,000,000. Although this will provide you substantially higher protection, the annual premium is modest (e.g., $150-$200 per year). We feel it is a worthwhile investment to provide peace of mind and to insulate your assets from a large liability claim.

ESTATE PLANNING

As with your investments, your wills should be reviewed periodically to make sure they fit your needs. Since your wills have not been reviewed in a number of years, we suggest you undertake such a review with your attorney. There have been significant changes in this area during the last few years. For example, it is now possible to leave all your assets to your spouse with no federal estate tax consequences.

While your wills may have been appropriate when they were executed, they may not be appropriate to your current situation. Therefore, a review of your estate plan appears advisable. Such a review should include not only your will but also your beneficiary designations and payment options for insurance policies and retirement plans.

LIABILITY MANAGEMENT

In addition to managing your assets, managing your liabilities is an important element of your financial life. The prudent use of leverage can help you increase your net worth. Changes in the tax law restricting the deduction for interest will become effective in 1987. This change will need to be analyzed for your particular needs. In the right circumstances, leveraging and borrowing often present desirable opportunities, but they are definitely not for the unwary. Your Financial Consultant can show you ways you might be able to use these options.

Borrow Cash Value of Life Insurance Policy

The cash value in your life insurance policies is estimated at $4,500. If these policies were purchased a number of years ago, it is probable that you can borrow the cash value at an interest rate of 5% or 6%. Reinvesting the proceeds at a higher rate would result in an overall financial gain. As part of our analysis, we have shown the borrowing of the cash values and reinvestment in more appropriate vehicles.

Personal Review
O · U · T · L · I · N · E

Loans Against Equity In Your Residence

A potential source of credit is your residence which is valued at about $225,000 with an outstanding mortgage of $120,000. The $105,000 difference represents the equity which can be used as collateral for borrowing. This equity can be tapped by using the Key Client Credit Account.

Unlike a conventional second mortgage, the Key Client Credit Account is a credit line that lets you borrow funds simply by making a phone call. You pay interest charges only on the funds you use. The interest rate is 1.5% above the prime rate and the repayment schedule is flexible, allowing you to pay interest only during the term of the loan. The principal can be due at maturity. It appears that you could qualify for a $48,700 line of credit.

As you may know, the new tax law has restricted the deductibility of mortgage interest if the amount borrowed exceeds the original purchase price of your residence plus the costs of home improvements. Interest on home loans for medical or educational expenses, however, are not subject to this limitation.

We have outlined several ways for you to borrow at an interest rate that is probably less than charged on a conventional loan. Managing your credit is an important element in your financial life. However, you must examine your comfort level with borrowing to determine whether this is a suitable strategy for you. Since your ability to get a loan may be as simple as writing a check, you must evaluate your financial ability to make timely payments on the debt.

Personal Review
O · U · T · L · I · N · E

SUMMARY

The charts below summarize how your assets are presently allocated and how your portfolio would change after our recommendations have been implemented. We have tried to structure your assets to meet your goals and objectives based on your current situation. Achieving your financial objectives is an ongoing process that needs to be closely monitored and adjusted to changing conditions. Your Financial Consultant, Doug Kalish, can help design an investment strategy that is appropriate for your needs.

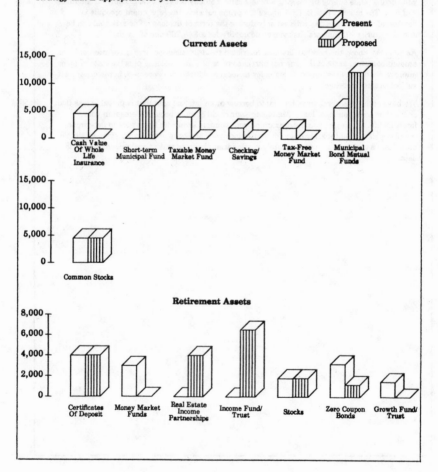

12 Six Families

Every family has a different financial story, especially under the new tax laws.

After making a luncheon speech one day to a women's professional group, I was stopped by a young lady who pulled me aside to relate some rather personal financial information.

"I'm 22 years old, I've just inherited an $80,000 home and $100,000, and I don't even know how to balance my checkbook," she said in an almost mournful tone. "What do you suggest I do?"

A less noble individual might have suggested that she meet him at the international wing of a major airport with a valise full of money and two tickets to Rio de Janeiro. Instead, I made a few suggestions about getting her financial act together. One can only imagine how distraught she might have been had she received her inheritance closer to the enactment of the perplexing new tax laws.

Because the new laws do not affect every individual or family the same way, everyone must come up with unique answers to the taxing questions. For some folks, tax changes mean big smiles, while for others it means heading for the pain-relievers in the medicine cabinet.

Following are some examples of different results of tax

changes for various Americans and some advice on making the proper investment and tax-planning decisions to cope with them effectively.

Case No. 1: Good news for Diana Brenner, single with no children

Diana, 25, rents an apartment and makes $22,000 a year as a bookkeeper. She puts $2,000 in an individual retirement account each year. Diana won't need to do much bookwork to notice some positive changes under the new tax laws. Her standard deduction benefit will be $2,540 in 1987 and $3,000 in 1988. Exemptions will grow from $1,080 in 1986 to $1,900 in 1987 and $1,950 in 1988. Because of all this largesse, Diana's taxable income will decrease from $18,920 in 1986 to $15,560 in 1987 and $15,050 in 1988.

So her tax liability will decrease from $2,788 in 1986 to $2,262 in 1987 and $2,258 in 1988. At the same time, she'll happily drop from a marginal tax rate of 23 percent in 1986 to 15 percent from then on.

Advice. To make the most from the benefits she'll receive from the new tax laws, Diana should continue to put money into her fully-deductible IRA early each year. She should also look into a 401(k) income deferral plan if available where she works. It is important to begin a regular systematic savings program, perhaps weekly or monthly, beginning with a bank account, money market fund or a growth stock mutual fund. Socking away tax savings would be a good start. She should keep track of expenses and, after building an emergency fund of three to six months' expenses, buying a home is an excellent long-range goal.

Case No. 2: Troy and Rachael Gaines, married with two children, can smell the roses

Both Troy, 38, and Rachael, 30, work. They own their own home, file taxes jointly and have a seven-year-old daughter and a four-year-old son. Troy earns $30,000 annually as a police officer, while Rachael makes $21,000 as a legal aide. Both will find the tax laws on their side. They'll have dividends of $200 in 1987 and $200 in 1988, as well as $800 in interest income in 1986, 1987 and 1988. So their total income will be $51,800 in 1986, rising to $52,000 in 1987 and 1988. They put $2,000 into a fully-deductible IRA in 1986 but will deduct just $200 in both 1987 and 1988. Their company 401(k) contributions remain constant at $3,000 in 1986, 1987 and 1988. Due to tax changes, they'll receive a two wage-earner deduction in 1986 only. That makes their adjusted gross income $44,700 in 1986, moving on up to $48,800 in 1987 and 1988.

The Gaines family has a number of itemized deductions, such as $6,000 in mortgage interest each year. Their deductible consumer interest will be phased out under tax changes, going from $500 in 1986 to $325 in 1987 and $200 in 1988. Real estate tax deductions remain constant at $2,000. The deduction for state and local sales taxes was $500 in 1986 but will disappear under the new laws. Troy and Rachael make $400 in charitable contributions each year and their miscellaneous deductions were $600 in 1986. The family's total itemized deductions were $10,000 in 1986, decreasing to $8,725 in 1987 and $8,600 in 1988 in the new scheme of taxation. Income after deductions was $34,700 in 1986, increasing to $40,075 in 1987 and $40,200 in 1988. Their zero-bracket amount was $3,670 in 1986. Exemptions were $4,320 in 1986, increasing to $7,600 in 1987 and $7,800 in 1988.

So, thanks to the tax changes, the Gaines family's taxable income decreases from $34,050 in 1986 to $32,475 in 1987 and

$32,400 in 1988. Their tax liability decreases from $5,660 in 1986 to $5,333 in 1987 and $5,205 in 1988, their tax bracket remaining constant at 28 percent.

Advice. The Gaines family should consider the non-deductible IRA, since it still puts the investor ahead of a normal investment even if the money is pulled out and penalties are paid after about 12 years. Look into 401(k) income deferral at work, which can shelter $7,000 annually. Begin an investment program to include growth stock funds.

The family should consider redeploying some assets into tax-free municipal bonds or tax-deferred annuities to blunt the tax bite. A college fund should be set aside for each child, keeping in mind that a child may earn up to $1,000 annually before tax is imposed at the parent's rates. The new stripped municipal bonds are a zero-coupon instrument that comes due in one to eight years, though there are longer-term zeroes available as well.

The family should pay off as much consumer debt as possible, since high interest charges look particularly bad when compared to the modest yields offered by many investments these days. Another possibility for the children's education might be a home equity loan, which could also be used to wipe out other consumer loans no longer tax-advantaged. But they shouldn't enter into that lightly, because increasing the debt load on a home could have unpleasant results unless discipline is used.

Case No. 3: Darrell and Marie Carvelli, married, children grown, will receive some pain, some gain

Darrell, 55, and Marie, 51, own a condominium and have no more mortgage payments. Darrell makes $56,000 a year as a sales representative, while Marie earns $15,000 as a part-time receptionist. They won't be totally sold on tax reform's results. Their dividends were $800 in 1986, increasing to $1,000 in 1987 and 1988. Interest income is $1,000 for all three years. Their total income was $72,800 for 1986, and will be $73,000 in both 1987 and 1988. They made a $4,000 IRA contribution for 1986, but don't have that deduction in 1987 or 1988. Their two wage-earner deduction for 1986 was $1,500. Adjusted gross income was $67,300 in 1986, growing to $73,000 in 1987 and 1988.

The Carvelli's consumer interest deduction in 1986 was $100, falling to $65 in 1987 and $40 in 1988. Their real estate tax deduction remains $2,500. State and local sales tax deduction was $800 in 1986. Deduction for state and local income taxes remains the same at $1,600, as does their $1,500 annual charitable contribution deductions. Miscellaneous deductions were $1,000 in 1986. This brings total itemized deductions to $7,500 in 1986, declining to $5,665 in 1987 and $5,640 in 1988. Income after deductions was $59,800 in 1986, increasing to $67,335 in 1987 and $67,360 in 1988. Their zero-bracket amount was $3,670 in 1986. Exemptions were $2,160 in 1986, rising significantly to $3,800 in 1987 and $3,900 in 1988.

Therefore, the couple's taxable income which was $61,310 in 1986 will increase to $63,535 in 1987 and then slip to $63,460 in 1988. Their tax liability of $15,062 in 1986 will increase to $15,327 in 1987 and then decline to $13,901 in 1988. They will go from a 38 percent marginal tax rate to 35 percent in 1987 and 28 percent in 1988.

Advice. Taking out a mortgage on the condominium might be worth considering by the Carvelli's, so they'll be able to deduct the interest. That, of course, depends on whether the family's psyche can handle the reintroduction of that debt. Other possibilities might be the movement of investments from taxable to tax-free choices such as municipal bonds. They should start setting money aside to prepare for retirement and consider a 401(k) plan and non-deductible IRA. Marie should look into the possibility of opening a Keogh plan. A single-premium whole life policy permits borrowing on a policy, often without interest expense. Series EE U.S. Savings Bonds are a good tax-deferral strategy.

A charitable lead trust, which is an irrevocable trust in which the individual gifts the principal or interest to a favorite charity, is another strategy. The family should pay off consumer loans and try to defer income into future years when its tax bracket will be lower.

Case No. 4: Robert and Marion Martinez, married, one wage-earner, will see taxes rise, then fall

Robert, 54, earns $130,000 as a dentist. He and wife Marion, who own their own home and have no children, will eventually be smiling about the new tax laws. They have an annual loss from rental property of $13,500, with their total income $116,500. They made a $2,250 IRA contribution in 1986, but will not make one in 1987 or 1988. Their company 401(k) contribution was $13,000 in 1986 but will drop to $7,000 due to tax changes. Their adjusted gross income of $101,250 in 1986 will increase to $109,500 for 1987 and 1988.

Their mortgage interest deduction will remain $8,000, and the real estate tax deduction remains $4,000. State and local sales tax deduction in 1986 was $2,000. State and local income taxes are $2,400 annually, and charitable contributions total $2,600 annually. Miscellaneous deductions in 1986 were $1,500. This means the Martinez' total itemized deductions of $20,500 in 1986 will decrease to $17,000. Income after deductions in 1986 of $80,750 will rise to $92,500 annually. Their zero-bracket amount in 1986 was $3,670. Exemptions go from $2,160 in 1986 to $3,800 in 1987 and $3,900 in 1988.

As a result, the Martinez family's taxable income of $82,260 will grow to $88,700 in 1987 before declining to $88,600 in 1988. Their tax liability of $23,723 in 1986 will increase to $24,135 in 1987 and decrease to $21,776 in 1988. Their marginal tax rate will go from 42 percent to 35 percent and wind up at 33 percent.

Advice. Because they have rental property, under tax changes the Martinez family should now find a "matched" program with passive income to offset present income. This might, for example, involve buying a parking lot, a program structured around 100 percent equity real estate or the funding of a movie or a play. Municipal bonds, single-premium whole life insurance and annuities should be considered, as well as a non-deductible IRA contribution.

Case No. 5: Ed and Bertha O'Mara, retired on fixed pension, will be on a bumpy track

Ed and Bertha, both 65, receive a pension of $12,500 a year from Ed's previous job as a railroad engineer. Their standard deduction benefit will be $6,200 starting in 1987 and 1988. Exemptions go from $4,320 in 1986 to $3,800 in 1987 and $3,900 in 1988.

Taxable income will decline from $8,180 in 1986 to $2,500 in 1987 and $2,400 in 1988. So the O'Mara's tax liability will drop from $519 in 1986 to $275 in 1987, before settling at $360 in 1988. They'll travel from a 12 percent tax bracket to 11 percent and wind up at 15 percent.

Advice. A bank certificate of deposit, high-yield bond fund, Ginnie Mae fund or balanced stock fund might be investment possibilities. The goal should be the highest taxable income possible, because of the O'Mara's low bracket. Diversity is important and something people who have worked hard for their money tend to forget. Part-time work might be one possibility for this couple to improve their financial status.

Case No. 6: Mitchell and Rita Thurber, high-income couple, tossed rudely out of their shelter

Mitchell, 44, and Rita, 40, have two children. He earns $150,000 a year as a divorce attorney. What happens to them under the new tax laws may shake their own marriage. Their net dividends of $2,300 in 1986 will increase to $2,500 in 1987 and 1988. Their interest income will remain constant at $7,500. Their short-term capital gains will average $6,000 each year. Really hurting will be the fact that their losses from partnerships will decline from $65,000 in 1986, to $42,250 in 1987 and $26,000 in 1988. This will boost their total income sky-high from $100,800 in 1986, to $123,750 in 1987 and $140,000 in 1988. They made an IRA contribution in 1986, but don't intend to from now on. Their $10,000 annual 401(k) plan contribution will shrink to $7,000 under tax changes. Their gross income of $88,800 in 1986 will rise to $116,750 in 1987 and $133,000 in 1988.

As far as itemized deductions are concerned, their $8,000 home mortgage interest will remain the same, but their consumer interest deduction will slip from $4,000 in 1986 to $2,600 in 1987 and $1,600 in 1988. Real estate taxes remain $3,500. Their $2,000 state and local sales tax deduction of 1986 is gone. State and local income tax deductions remain at $1,600, and charitable contribution deductions stay at $3,000. Miscellaneous deductions drop from $3,500 in 1986 to $1,165 in 1987 and $840 in 1988. Which means that total itemized deductions drop from $25,600 in 1986 to $19,865 in 1987 to $18,540 in 1988. Income after deductions skyrockets from $63,200 in 1986 to $96,885 in 1987 and $114,460 in 1988. Zero-bracket amount in 1986 was $3,670. Exemptions rise from $4,320 in 1986 to $7,600 in 1987 and $7,800 in 1988.

As a result, tax reform really throws the book at the Thurbers. Their taxable income of $62,550 in 1986 zooms to $89,285 in 1987 and $106,660 in 1988. Tax liability grows from $15,533 in 1986 to $24,340 in 1987 and $27,736 in 1988. Their marginal rate slides from 38 percent to 35 percent to 33 percent.

Advice. Passive income shelters should be set up, college funds placed in their teen-aged children's names, and dividends and income moved into tax-exempt and tax-deferred vehicles. In many cases, existing shelter deals will be restructured by those who syndicated them, and the Thurbers would be fortunate to have that happen to them. A "ladder" of tax-free bonds or unit trusts coming due in different years is a popular strategy. A home equity loan might be another possibility, as would a charitable lead trust. The family should pay off all consumer debt!

Did you find yourself among these families? If so, you now know whether you'll make out like a bandit under the new tax laws or were robbed. In some cases the situation is tougher than others, but by working out your situation and making judicious use of the investments and strategies explained in this book, you too can make money with the new tax laws.

Tax Work Sheet

	1986	Current year
Income		
Wages, salary, etc.	_____	_____
Interest income	_____	_____
Dividends	_____	_____
Capital gains	_____	_____
Rent, partnerships	_____	_____
Unemployment compensation	_____	_____
All other income	_____	_____
Total income	_____	_____
Adjustments		
Employee business expense	(____)	████
IRA deduction	(____)	(____)
Married couple both work	(____)	████
Keogh plan deduction	(____)	(____)
Other adjustments	(____)	(____)
Adjusted gross income	_____	_____
Deductions		
Medical and dental	_____	_____
State and local income, property, personal property tax	_____	_____
State and local sales tax	_____	████
Mortgage interest	_____	_____
Other interest	_____	_____
Charitable contributions	_____	_____
Casualty and theft losses	_____	_____
Miscellaneous deductions	_____	_____
Total deductions	_____	
minus standard deduction	(____)	████
Allowed itemized deductions	(____)	(____)

13   Lifetime Strategies

Always have a financial strategy for each stage of your life, one flexible enough to cope with anything tax laws or a changing economy can dish out.

The bumper sticker on the shiny new motor home pulling onto the interstate highway got the message across succinctly. In big block letters were the words: "Our children's inheritance."

The Albert Brooks film "Lost in America" featured comedian Brooks in a frenzy when his fellow-yuppie wife gambled away their lifesavings in Las Vegas. Worst of all, he explained, her actions had "violated the nestegg."

Your money concerns do vary with the time in your life. Millions of Americans talk constantly of what they should have done with their money when they were younger, or how much more they could do now if they only had more money to play around with. But it isn't just the 80-year-old couple stashing money under the mattress that's missing out on greater returns. Younger folks make their own foolish mistakes with a dollar, and it's important to have a timeline of changing investments throughout your life.

The growing ranks of single Americans, for example, have flashier cars, better stereos, nicer vacations and decidedly worse finances than their married counterparts. The problem is too much impulse and too little stability in their money planning. "Since I was able to buy a $700 video cassette recorder for $500, I guess my ability to shrewdly handle money goes without saying," quipped Carol, a 27-year-old professional who admits her handling of personal finance is less than professional. Or as Jack, a 35-year-old salesman, puts it: "I enjoy myself and manage to pay my bills—some of them actually on time."

More people are single these days, and more of them are staying single. While many do take control of their financial futures, others are so busy with work and recreation that they set few goals. What they don't spend is automatically stashed in money market funds or checking accounts without considering alternatives. Single people often don't save enough money, operating under the misconception that it isn't necessary until they're married. Those who expect to remain single use it as an excuse to never save money at all.

It's important for those going it alone to make financial plans, because there's no one else to depend on. A single person should first set aside 10 percent of gross income in savings and investments each month. An amount equal to three to six months of expenses should be kept in an emergency fund. Because singles often have more discretionary income than married couples but less control, it helps to have a basic budget that limits monthly expenses for eating out, entertainment and clothing. With deductions for consumer credit being phased out, it also makes sense to cut back on debt. It is a consistent problem of single people.

Next, take some chances. Growth stocks of smaller companies and stock mutual funds permit rapid growth of your investment, even though they also carry a chance of decline. No one is dependent upon you, so you can be as aggressive as you like without anyone scolding you or saying, "I told you so." Buying property is one of the few ways to ease the tax bite and, despite worries of being tied down, is still worthwhile for a single person. Tax-exempt investments such as municipal bonds or bond funds could also be a portion of a personal portfolio. Diversification of investments, no matter how small the amount, is always important for a single person, whether it involves stocks, bank accounts or real estate.

Though a single person might consider one of the new types of insurance policies that provide not only a death benefit but a chance to defer income without paying taxes now, for the most part he shouldn't worry so much about life insurance as health and disability insurance. Check out group coverage offered through work and make sure the overall coverage from this and supplementary policies is sufficient. Go over pension benefits and find out when you're vested and whether your benefits are adequate. People often don't read the fine print or realize that restrictions vary a great deal from company to company. Look into company profit-sharing and 401(k) income deferral plans.

These days women have become a major force in investing. The rapidly increasing ranks of women investors are a major reason behind an overall rise in the number of individual American stockholders. Once overlooked by investment institutions, women lately have become favored targets of an endless array of mailings, advertisements and seminars. Sophistication of the promotions may vary, but all share a desire to attract the dollars of this growing market segment. The stakes are impressive; 57 percent of all new stock investors these days are women, according to a study commissioned by the New York Stock Exchange. More of the women investors these days are executives who have decided to take their own finances in hand without waiting for a husband to do it for them one day. Some also say they've learned a lesson from seeing their mothers left without a firm grasp of investments, following either the death of their spouse or divorce. According to the NYSE study, the typical new female investor is 34 years old, married and holding a professional or technical job. Average portfolio size is $2,200 and average family income is

$35,000. The nation's overall stock holdings, not just those of new investors, are an even 50-50 split between men and women.

Money and investment often have been topics of heated debate between the sexes. Who holds the purse strings and who knows about family finances varies from household to household, as does the issue of whether daughters are made privy to the same financial instruction as sons. There remain a few subtle differences among attitudes of women and men investors, say the experts, though such differences are based primarily on confidence. In the past, some women making initial forays into the male-dominated investment world have received condescending treatment from brokers attuned to the "old days." Those were the days when men held all the money—except when they died and left it to their spouses.

A real problem women investors have is that they keep apologizing for asking perfectly valid questions about investments, according to a number of financial planners whose clients are predominantly women. "The only other difference I've found is that women are far less willing to go with a 'hot tip' than men are, preferring to seek further information first," said one.

Based upon the experiences of my investment column, I have some wholly inconclusive observations about financial attitudes among men and women. Women investors do ask more questions or at least often have the responsibility of asking questions for their households. Nearly three-fourths of the hundreds of reader letters from around the country that I receive for my "question-and-answer" column are written by women. About half of these say they are writing on behalf of their husband and themselves. Married women seem to defer to their spouses on financial matters whenever questions are asked in public. When I open the floor to questions after an investment talk to a community or professional group, in the vast majority of instances the husband will pose the question. Regardless of the demographics of income or professional status of the audience, the wife rarely asks about financial matters for a couple.

But, thankfully, things are changing. Financial planners tell me that, while older women investors are likely to say that their husbands invested their money in a certain way and that they intend to do the same, that's definitely not the case with younger women. It's a big difference, with younger women basing their own decisions not only on professional advice, but what they've learned by following financial sections of newspapers and various investment periodicals and books.

Single investors and women investors have their specific considerations. And money considerations don't necessarily become easy once one gives up the single life and gets married.

Many thoroughly modern working couples are achievers on the job but as bewildered as Dagwood and Blondie when they try to manage those two paychecks at home. There's little coordination and plenty of tension over who's spending what. Either one paycheck is tossed around as "funny money" or monthly expenditures are pushed beyond even the limit of the combined salaries. "I like to spend a whole lot more than my wife does," admits one spouse familiar with money disagreements. "I'd take off on a vacation trip every other month and be willing to buy a different car every year, but she puts the clamps on. I guess it's good that she's tougher."

Many couples are made up of two distinct personalities: a spender and a saver. Neither personality is linked to any one gender exclusively. Try to understand each other's attitude toward both spending and saving. It's a good idea to divide up the financial duties from time to time so that each has a shot at writing the checks and seeing what bills must be paid. Otherwise, one spouse will inevitably be asking for money and wondering why the other is being stingy, while the "stingy" one will view the other as a spendthrift. Earmark money for specific goals and, in the event one salary is substantially less than the other, monitor it carefully so it isn't frittered away. The biggest problem with two-income families is that they spend all their money, not realizing that layoffs, career changes, children or even a death can radically change their financial situation. Even though most working couples today intend to keep on working, they should at least keep in mind the potential of one day having to live off one salary.

While it's always been considered a good idea to try to use one paycheck to cover necessities and the other for savings and discretionary purchases, every couple must come up with their own plan. Many still pool everything, but there is an increasing trend toward two individual accounts with a percentage of each income going into a third joint account for general housekeeping. However money is handled, each spouse should be well informed of the total financial picture and capable of handling finances on his or her own. Death or divorce has left many an uninformed spouse barely capable of balancing a checkbook. With the divorce rate as high as it is, more working couples are keeping a joint account but handling individually many of their investments and clothing expenses. This practice is even more common in second marriages.

Taxes are obviously an important consideration. If couples haven't been married long or have received substantial raises, they often don't withhold enough tax from their paychecks and may wind up owing thousands of dollars to the government. Each spouse should have at least one credit card bearing his or her own name, in order to establish a separate long-term credit identity. It's also a good idea to purchase a car in one's own name. Go over group insurance coverage for each spouse. At some companies, a "cafeteria-style" approach is offered. That means that, rather than duplicating the coverage of the other spouse, different fringe benefits that complement each other may be chosen instead. Also set a goal of setting aside savings of as close to 10 percent of combined income as possible.

Middle age can be a perplexing time when it comes to personal finances. Education of children is often a major goal and income is important. Blue-chip stocks featuring both dividend income and some potential growth in price are good choices. Like high-yield bonds and certificates of deposit, they provide current income and solid return if cashed in to meet those family needs. Municipal bonds can be a good choice if there is substantial family income to be sheltered from federal taxes. If you're still interested in stock mutual funds, move out of the go-go funds of your younger years into more balanced funds. Consider possibilities such as company thrift or profit-sharing plans, as well as annuities.

At some point during middle age, a person will at last be free of responsibilities for children's education, while retirement still seems an awfully long way off. But self-control is still important. "Once the kids are gone, people typically decide they owe themselves something and opt for a vacation in which they spend a lot more than they need to spend, or they decide to treat themselves to a car a lot more expensive than necessary," said Ben C. Baldwin, certified financial planner with Equitable Financial Services in Northbrook, Ill. "That's understandable, but you really shouldn't go on a binge as some people do. Life spans are much longer now and money has to last." It's important for those facing middle age to adjust to having more money around, while at the same time raise the sophistication of their basic investments.

Investing is a challenge for senior citizens these days, too. You see, choices just aren't what they used to be. Just ask members of the finance club for seniors that meets each week at Mayer Kaplan Jewish Community Center in Skokie, Ill. Idell Schatz, who for years ignored any yield less than double digit, now says she'd "jump" for far less. Declines in interest rates on bank certificates of deposit, added Ben Lanz, "means many retirees have seen their income drop 50 percent." And Rose Abrams, once confident about investing in the high-yield electric utility stocks, acknowledges that recent worries about nuclear power have left her "very cautious."

Based on hundreds of letters received by my investment column, it's the same coast to coast. These are confusing times for folks trying to live off their investment income and avoid digging into principal. One problem is that many seniors look for one pat answer. They shift their entire portfolio from one investment to another as conditions change, without building necessary diversity into their holdings. Whether senior citizens have $5,000 or $5 million, their primary concern is safety of principal and providing for the surviving spouse. When you don't diversify, you run the risk of interest rates or market fluctuations having a devastating effect on your investments.

As an important part of any senior investment, Jack Haggerty, vice president with Prudential-Bache Securities, suggests CDs of 1- to 5-year maturities, staggering those maturities so money will be coming due and available regularly. Haggerty's model senior portfolio would put 50 to 60 percent of the money in investments such as CDs, Treasury securities, AAA-rated bonds and Ginnie Mae funds. Another 25 percent should go either into high-quality stocks or conservative stock funds. Ten percent of the portfolio should be placed in a liquid account with a bank or money market fund. The rest of the money he'd put into speculative stocks or an income-producing partnership.

Retirees often invest in the highest-yield electrical utilities, not realizing that higher yield means a utility has greater risk. In recent times, it has made more sense for a senior to steer clear of utilities with nuclear projects in the works. Take a slightly lower yield to observe greater safety of dividend and stock price. While seniors with considerable retirement income would do well with municipal bonds and bond funds, seniors with little investment income sometimes put money in such tax-free choices simply because they hate to pay tax. They'd be better off with a higher yield.

Take advantage of any available senior discounts, such as free checking at your bank or special deals on vacation air travel. Other discounts worth considering are:

  — A $5 annual membership fee in the 21-million-member American Association of Retired Persons, 1909 K Street N.W., Washington, D.C., 20049, offers discounts such as hotels, rental cars, catalog pharmacy items and an auto club. Members must be 50 or older.

— A $7.50 annual fee to the Sears, Roebuck & Co.-sponsored Mature Outlook program, Allstate Plaza, Northbrook, Ill., 60062, provides similar discounts but also includes discounts on some Sears products and half-percent off on car and boat financing. Members must be 50 or older.

— The Silver Pages publication produced by Southwestern Bell, Suite 407, 1625 Des Peres Rd., St. Louis, Mo., 63131, is offered free to those 60 and older in 16 states. It lists local discounts in areas such as banking, dental care, travel and products.

Whatever your age, keep in mind the importance of proper budgeting. For most Americans, formulating a personal financial budget and following it is about as enjoyable as visiting the dentist or going on a crash weight-loss program. Yet by taking the time to figure out where your money should go, versus where it does go, you'll be a lot further along in meeting all the goals you've set for yourself and your family.

Begin by tracking your spending and income carefully over a three-month period. Write down all the money you spend in a small notebook you carry with you, since it's easy to lose track, especially when cashing an extra $10 check at the grocery store. Cash is often the biggest gap in reconstructing your expenses, for it can add up to a couple of thousand dollars a year.

List all of your income sources, such as wages after deductions, in a basic family budget book, generally available in stationary stores. Don't include bonuses, profit-sharing payments or special dividends until you're sure of them. Don't subtract any voluntary deductions from your paycheck, such as donations to charity or health-insurance premiums because you can still control those expenditures.

Write down all expenses, not just the obvious ones such as mortgage and car payments, but also the less obvious ones that can be traced through purchase receipts and charge-account payments. Long-term debt, such as a mortgage, ideally should be no more than 25 to 35 percent of gross income, although some financial planners are raising that amount because mortgage debt is one of the few tax breaks left. The next largest expense is usually food, followed by transportation, medical costs and clothing. If you're able to save 10 percent of your gross salary, you're doing a terrific job. Short-term debt, such as credit-card purchases, should also be well under control.

Totaling your incoming and outgoing expenses will result in a cash-flow statement. If you had an operating surplus of, say, $2,000 last year, your net worth should have increased by at least that much. A negative income statement isn't good, but don't lose sleep if it's the result of unusual difficulties as opposed to deep-seated financial mistakes. Once you've figured out your cash flow, use it to set your priorities and outline a budget that adheres to what you wish to spend and also permits some saving for the future. Estimate how much you can put directly into savings each month, and do it faithfully. Allow some flexibility for the unexpected, such as additional medical costs or car repairs.

Determine which of your expenditures may be out of line, such as spending too much money on dining out. Keep better track of your weaknesses, monitoring your budget each week and going over the figures in depth every six months. Be realistic in your plan, so your budget doesn't simply wind up in a drawer collecting dust. It's a good idea to list at the first of each year exactly what you want to buy during the year, such as two new suits, a plant for the house or new furniture, as well as how much you wish to put aside for major goals. With your priorities set in a budget, you can buy what you need when you have the money, rather than impulsively buying things you don't really want.

Figuring your net worth is also important. How much an individual or family is "worth" in financial terms usually is a juicy topic of whispered gossip, not open conversation. Neighbors or relatives speculate with raised eyebrows about a family's bottom line each time they observe some extravagance. That might be a fancy car in the driveway or reports of an expensive vacation to some exotic paradise. But the family secret is probably safe: the objects of that speculation probably don't know how much they're really worth in dollars and cents, either. Surprisingly, financial planners at New York's Citibank say that 90 percent of the time the individual finds out he's worth much more than he thought he was.

A personal net worth worksheet consists of the following:

—*What you own.* Total up your assets, which include cash, checking accounts, savings accounts and certificates of deposit; money market accounts; U.S. savings bonds; bonds at current market value; individual retirement accounts or Keogh funds; cash value of life insurance; vested amount in company benefits such as deferred profit-sharing; stock purchase plans, company savings plans or accrued pension benefits; current market value of an owned home and other real estate; car; personal assets such as antiques, paintings, jewelry, furs or a boat; shares in a business or partnership; loans you are owed; estates or trusts.

—*What is owed.* Your total liabilities include current bills for credit cards, utilities or medical expenses; installment loans for cars, appliances or home improvements; total owed on mortgages; insurance policy loans; tuition loans; taxes due this year on federal, state and local income; taxes due on total property; other debts.

—*The difference.* Subtract your total liabilities from your total assets; that difference is your net worth. While all of this may seem like a Herculean task, it needn't be if you are methodical. Start with the most readily available information, such as current bank statement, passbook and money market fund statement. If some of your stocks aren't listed in the newspaper, check with a broker. The cash value of your life insurance may be printed on your annual premium statement.

Consult real estate agents about what homes similar to yours are selling for in the neighborhood—also a good move if you ever contest the property valuation put upon your home for tax purposes. If you think your home has appreciated a great deal, ask your bank to recommend a professional appraiser you could hire for an evaluation. If you held a quick sale of your home furnishings and clothing, how much could you get? You'll have to estimate on the low side. Check with friends who recently held garage sales.

When figuring value of personal possessions such as antiques, jewelry or art, don't let your sentimental attachment enter into it. You may want to hire a professional appraiser. To set a value on your car, check the trade-in figures that car dealers follow for used cars. More employees are building equity in company fringe benefit plans, but figure in only the vested benefits that actually belong to you, not those based on meeting certain conditions later on. In the category of debts, add up unpaid balances on all the debts you make payments on. Check your periodic mortgage statement indicating balance owed. Do the same with credit card bills. Include insurance premiums due this year, as well as any other contractual payments. Include installments due on your estimated income tax and school and other property taxes due.

All of this requires homework, but it may be worth it to find out you are worth more than you think. Even if you aren't, you should know. Leave the speculation to the neighbors. Know your financial worth so that you can make intelligent plans for both your investments and your tax-paying.

As you move along the timeline of investments, children obviously play a major role. Spending money on them and helping them understand the importance of handling money effectively are both major tasks. Children and money go hand in hand, starting with the costs of baby care, progressing to the learning of the financial facts of life and often winding up with a hefty tab for a college education.

Bringing up Baby is expensive, yet many families don't take the time to figure out the costs they'll encounter. After mentally preparing themselves to give up free time and make room for the new arrival, they don't do as much financial planning for this lifelong commitment as they would for a vacation or a new car. First-time parents, whether overindulgent or stingy, always wind up spending more than they think they will. They face the task of keeping costs in line now so the youngster will one day have the money necessary for important goals, such as a quality education.

"I don't think you can ever really account for every expense beforehand, because if there's a toy our daughter really wants, we're likely to get it for her," said Karen, whose first-born is 18 months old. "But my husband and I mostly have splurged on items that involve her personal safety, such as her car seat and furniture."

Here are estimated expenses for a child's first 18 months, based on the experiences of families at several income levels:

- Maternity clothing can be a substantial expense the first time around: $700.

- Hospital birth costs depend on insurance coverage, but your noncovered expenses can be significant: $1,000.

- Pediatrician costs vary, but even minor ailments drive them up: $900.

- Clothing totals are affected by gifts or hand-me-downs you receive: $1,400.

- Furniture and accessories for a nursery run the gamut from basic to designer styles: $1,000.

- Diapers, particularly the disposable kind, can cost you more than $10 a week: $900.

- Formula costs vary, and baby food expenses depend on whether you buy store brands or make it at home: $1,000.

- Toy purchases are based on how fancy or generous you wish to be. Remember, many youngsters still prefer to play with the box the toys come in: $800.

- Baby-sitting costs depend on how much time you

want away from your little angel, but even one night
a week could cost $15. Grandma and Grandpa prob-
ably have a cheaper rate: $900.

— Total estimated cost of the first 18 months: $8,600.

Such costs vary widely and are open to dispute, with many
families paying far less, yet even the lowest possible figure
would take a big chunk out of a family budget. This also
doesn't take into account the money lost if one parent isn't
working for a while or the significant day-care expenses incurred if both parents are working. A highly liquid emergency
fund of at least three months' salary is crucial, whatever the
tally. In the case of a two-salary family, it is also important to
begin planning to live off one salary, even if it will only be
for a short period of time. Go over your life insurance coverage
to determine what benefits would be necessary to meet long-
term needs. Look into your disability coverage at work as well.
Within 30 days of the child's birth, redo wills and determine
the guardian and also trustees of funds for the child.

While you're footing the bill for your tyke, it's important
that you help educate that child about money matters. Helping a boy or girl understand what money really is and the best
ways of handling it is an important parental responsibility that
must start when the child is very young. It has little to do
with how much money a family actually has, but plenty to do
with the lifelong psychology behind spending and saving it.
"So many adults these days hold money over their spouse's
head because that's the way their parents held it over theirs,
or they've never learned how to spend sensibly without suf-
fering some sort of emotional trauma," said Jeanne I. Haf-
strom, associate professor of family and consumer economics
at the University of Illinois, Urbana-Champaign.

An early start at communicating a family financial value system and careful following of that system by the parents themselves can make the difference between a child growing up to
think money is an oppressive concept or a liberating one.
There is no one right way of teaching a child about money,

just as there is no one right way to rear a child. However, the experts offer some important considerations, even if you as a parent are able to do it successfully in an entirely different manner. Probably the best way for a child to learn how to handle money is by having an allowance and living within it. Even children have some fixed expenses such as lunches and flexible costs such as toys, and they can learn that money goes further with planned spending.

A small allowance may begin as early as four or five years of age if there are older children already receiving allowances and the concept is understood. More likely, six to eight years old is the time when children understand money is used to buy things and they can deal with delayed gratification. Decide on the size of the allowance by having family members discuss their individual needs and the family's basic needs, so the child will see that there are always limitations. Discuss what his money should be used for. Give the money at regular intervals, perhaps twice a week in the case of the youngest children, and be firm about saying "no" between those pay periods.

Children shouldn't be paid for basic chores around the home, since they must realize that those are just a part of being a member of the family, say many experts. Using this no-strings-attached philosophy, it is best to only pay for a chore if it is some special job that the family needs done and you'd otherwise have to pay someone else to do it. It's a big mistake to pay for good school grades, since it makes money rather than an education the goal. The biggest error parents make is holding money over a child's head and threatening to withhold it for various reasons. This attitude frequently carries over to adulthood, with money considered a club to wield over others.

When the child is very young, set shorter-term goals for allowance money, such as an inexpensive treat or toy. A costly purchase or a long-time aim such as an education may seem so far away that the child will lose interest altogether. However, when gift money is to be used for long-term goals, do try to explain the concept to the youngster. Whenever money is being spent, such as at the grocery store, a small child should have the concept explained to him. As the child reaches teen years, a small investment in a bank account, a mutual fund or a stock would further investment understanding. Part-time jobs during teen years help with work habits and money sense. Once goals of higher education are understood, the child can use money from jobs to help fund future tuition or living expenses.

The reality of finances and children hits home under the new tax laws, in which children's investment income over $1,000 gets taxed at the parent's bracket until age 14. As discussed earlier in this book, this requires greater financial planning, taking into account the entire family's income. Much of the family's preoccupation with financial planning, however, will relate to the costs of higher education. The price tag for a college education isn't all that cheap right now, requiring about $60,000 for tuition and living expenses at a major private college, $35,000 at a public institution. But calculations show that by the time today's bright-looking toddler graduates from college shortly after the turn of the century, it may cost $300,000 for four years at a private college. At less expensive institutions, it will probably mean $90,000 to $150,000. "Unfortunately, families often wait until the last couple of years before they finally think about education costs, or they start early but just put the money in low-rate passbook savings," said Roger Koester, financial analyst with the Northwestern University office of financial aid.

A rule of thumb among financial planners—probably an overly optimistic one—is that you should try to have the cost of a college education put aside, earning dividends until that future date.

Some investment possibilities include:

—*Zero-coupon bonds.* Available in a variety of different types, these deeply-discounted instruments, offering a calculated, face-value payout upon maturity, can provide a regimented payment plan for college. Tax-exempt zeroes should flourish under the new tax laws. Have various bonds come due each college year.

—*Growth stock mutual funds.* By investing with a firm that offers a "family" of funds, you can later switch into money market funds whenever the stock market is low and interest rates are high.

—*Stocks with growth potential.* Stock in quality firms that don't have heavy dividends to increase the family's tax burden is a good idea. Dividend reinvestment programs provide a means of easily adding to your holdings through regular deposits.

—*U.S. savings bonds.* No longer an outmoded investment, savings bonds now provide a competitive market-based rate that changes each six months. Payroll deduction plans help accumulate savings bonds, which defer income until you cash them in. It is particularly a good strategy to put money in savings bonds to be redeemed after the child reaches age 14 when the proceeds will be taxed at his own lower individual bracket.

As your youngster nears college, check out financial aid. Aid formulas take into consideration many factors, such as how many children are in college at one time, so even some comfortable middle-class families might qualify. Obviously outright gifts are the most popular, but there are also loans and work-study opportunities. The number of students who hold part-time jobs is on the rise at campuses around the nation, often totalling better than half the students. That's no surprise, of course. The bottom line cost of a college education is truly staggering.

There are some highly innovative programs to pay for college education. Pittsburgh's Duquesne University for $5,600 has permitted alumni and their relatives to buy four years at the university starting in 1999. It is then expected to be worth $52,000. In its early offering, the deal pulled in more than $3 million for the future education of nearly 500 students, so it has been broadened to include nonalumni. The goal is better than 2,000 prepaid students signed up during the 1980s. If the child doesn't wind up going to Duquesne, the family gets back the initial payment without interest. Many other universities are looking into the possibility of such a program as well. The University of Pennsylvania lets a family pay tuition for a youngster's total education up front, avoiding any hikes in tuition through graduation. Some universities are making below-market loan rates available to students, as are some states. It is always worthwhile to review a family's situation each year, for the fact of having more than one child in school at a time can affect the formulas used in giving financial aid.

Among federal loans, the National Direct Student Loan runs 10 years at 5 percent interest to a maximum of $3,000 per year and is primarily for families with income of less than $30,000. The Guaranteed Student Loan, also for 10 years, charges eight percent interest to a maximum of $2,500, and is also for families with less than $30,000 in income. A Payment Loan for Undergraduate Students is for 10 years at 12 percent interest up to a maximum of $3,000 and has no income restrictions.

Under the new tax laws, scholarships and fellowships granted after Aug. 16, 1986 are subject to new rules eliminating the tax-free status of aid spent for room, board and incidental expenses. Only aid for tuition, fees, books and laboratory equipment is now deductible.

Increasingly, it is expected that parents will be using home equity loans, which permit them to tap the equity built up in their home at a loan rate a point or two above the prime lending rate. Educational costs were specifically singled out as acceptable use for the proceeds of a home equity loan under tax revisions.

Obviously, tax laws play a big role in your goals of making money at various stages of your life. But you can carefully select the proper instruments to get what you want for you and your family whatever your age.

14   Modern Ideas

Modern ideas require some old-fashioned common sense.

It has, for example, been a big deal in recent years for professionals to brag to their friends that they've arrived because they're incorporated. That ego trip may no longer make sense, for the new tax laws make other alternatives a better bet.

With consumer interest being phased out as a deduction under the new tax laws, leasing, rather than buying, a car may no longer carry the stigma with many people that it once did.

Technology is another modern idea evident in the greater number of car telephones on our expressways. It, too, has its good and bad points. For example, Don, a young executive, is a hard charger who gets to work by 7 a.m. to get a jump on his work before the rush of telephone calls and meetings. That used to work just fine until his boss got a car cellular telephone. Don's life changed drastically. "He'll telephone me just as he leaves his house, ask me what's going on and chat for a half-hour or longer on his way into the office," Don groans. "I can't get a thing done."

Another modern idea, going into business for yourself, requires learning some good old-fashioned bookkeeping techniques that some folks never get around to mastering.

Buying a new-fangled computer may sound good, but unless you know what you need and learn how best to use it, your money would be better put in a lamp for the living room.

Beyond the tax considerations, there are pros and cons with either leasing or getting the best car financing deal. I recently heard an observer comment as a sleek silver BMW pulled out of the company parking lot: "Sure it looks nice, but I know him and he just leases it. I much prefer to own my car." Actually, a leased car looks no different from one owned by its driver. It's unlikely that any more than a few coworkers and friends know whether it's leased anyway. So, for many drivers these days, there's no longer a stigma attached to leasing. Leased cars account for more than 15 percent of the vehicles on the road and the numbers are growing rapidly. While many people would never lease under any circumstances, it does offer an alternative. By leasing, you don't have to pay as much up front and monthly payments are lower. You're also likely to lease a fancier car than you'd probably buy. When you build up equity in a leased car, you do have use of that extra money for the four years of the lease. Of course, how wisely you handle that money is up to you.

The trick is to lease a popular car, since the dealer will give you a better deal knowing he can make more money when he sells the car at the end of the lease. Leasing tends to be better for drivers who don't drive more than 15,000 miles each year, since that is when additional charges of 6 to 15 cents a mile typically kick in. "Remember that you can't back out of a lease easily, for you'll have to pay a substantial penalty," cautioned one dealer who also leases cars. "Also keep in mind that, if the car isn't in good condition when you turn it in at lease end, you'll have to pay for fixing it."

Leasing is popular among young professionals who'd rather have their money now. "I'd rather put that downpayment money toward my mortgage payments, and leasing makes that possible," said a young engineer whose wife, a nurse, also leases her car. First popular in California, leasing grew in other areas when cars rose greatly in price. "In the old days, when a car was $8,000, you didn't have to come up with much of a downpayment," said one dealer. "With the average price now $13,000, people are looking at bigger downpayments and monthly payments." An $11,000 Pontiac Grand Am would require a $2,000 downpayment if bought and financed, compared to putting down one month's payment if leased. Payments on a 48-month purchase contract would be $228 a month, while lease payments would be about $20 less. Resale on that Pontiac for an owner would be 40 percent at the end of four years. Always shop around. Some leases permit the driver no rights to the car at the end of the lease period, while others give the option to buy at the end of the lease. The option to buy the car often sets the purchase price in advance.

Even though buying a car isn't the same tax deal it was prior to the new tax laws, the modern cut-rate financing programs offered from time to time by carmakers anxious to clear their lots of inventory can deliver a good price. A super cut-rate loan can mean several thousand dollars less over the life of the car. It is important to realize that what matters is the final cost you wind up paying. Some dealers offering special financing will jack up the price of the car you're buying. Or they'll charge more for some options than they might otherwise. Sometimes the special deals are only on cars that just aren't selling, so you should investigate whether the reasons why it isn't selling will matter to you. It is a good idea to first go to your local bank or credit union to get a price on financing, then use that to compare the deal the cardealer is offering. Sometimes it is worthwhile to ask not only for quotes on prices that include the cardealer's financing, but to ask for a price quote based upon your obtaining alternate financing or paying cash for the car. In the case of a choice being given for either a cash rebate or lower-rate financing, it may make sense to take the rebate and then shop for a good bank loan rate to finance the car.

In recent days, several banks around the country have actually started offering adjustable-rate car loans that are tied to an index such as the prime lending rate. Typically, the rate can change every quarter. At a time when there are so many financial variables in our lives, making your car loan another one hardly seems like a good idea, unless your confidence about the future of interest rates is truly expansive.

The home computer is another modern idea that requires doing your homework. Despite grand predictions that the home computer would soon dramatically change the lives of American families, the reviews remain mixed. Much of this book was written on a home computer made by a major manufacturer. Several technical mishaps that occurred during the writing might have seemed minor to your average technician, but to this author loomed as tragic as another Chernobyl nuclear accident.

The Burns family of Silver Spring, Md., is a computer success story. Sid and Tammy brought home their computer four years ago and son Andy, now 14, took to it like a fish to water. He spent a month this summer in a special advanced computer course at Duke University. "Andy hardly ever watches television and is always in front of the computer, while our 10-year-old daughter Holly likes to play games on it," said Sid, an accountant. "The computer is giving them a big head start in life." But the McFarlands of Wilmette, Ill., didn't do as well. Bill, a minister, bought a $4,000 home computer on which to prepare his sermons, while Esther hoped to use it for bookkeeping. They had no knowledge of computers and it took a year of struggling before they could do much of anything with it. "People get in over their heads because of the marketing campaigns, not realizing these are business machines and not adult toys," said Bill. "If you drive a Mercedes, you can jump in and drive it because it drives just like a Chevy, but that's not the case with an advanced computer."

Most Americans still buy a home computer to educate their children and themselves about the computer world, sometimes starting out with inexpensive games. Moving on to more meaningful applications, families use a word processor for typing letters while the children use it for homework. Some track household finances by computer, and they're particularly helpful with a home business. There are subscription data base services that help investors follow the stock and bond markets, and also computerized home shopping services. A big problem that the makers of computers are trying to overcome is the fact that many types of computer software in the past haven't been so easy to use or didn't have useful applications. Less cumbersome word processing and easier home budget software are part of the move toward making computers more acceptable by average families. Of course, lower prices go a long way toward accomplishing the same end.

Slow orders, big losses and fierce competition in the troubled computer industry can mean a good deal for an individual willing to shop around. Just be careful and know what you're looking for. "Some families are led into stores by ads for $150 computers and wind up buying too little for their needs," said one officer of a local computer society. "They later find they must buy much more to do what they intended to do." There are wide price ranges. For example, a computer for games could cost $150 to $750. A disk drive might add $150 and individual software packages, which are the programs that tell the computer what to do, may cost $5 to $70 apiece. (Watch the prices on software, however, for some makers try to jack up prices when they come up with a program that appears particularly unique or popular.) For word processing and personal finance, you might pay $1,500 to $2,500 for the basic computer, add a printer for $300 to $1,000 and purchase software packages at $50 to $500 apiece. Overall, expect to pay around $600 for a modest unit, or as much as $4,000 at the high end, although prices are coming down month by month.

Before you buy a home computer, keep the following in mind:

> — Know what you intend to use the computer for and how much equipment you'll need. Research the software and make sure it isn't overly complicated or cumbersome. Determine your general price range.

— Do your homework by consulting the library and magazine stands for books and periodicals that explain computers and analyze various brands. Talk to friends who use home computers. Learn some of the computer jargon.

— Comparison shop by visiting at least three stores and watch for special sales. Choose a brand likely to be around a long time and that has extensive software available for it. Compare warranties and service. Ask about reasonably priced training classes and whether assistance is available by telephone should you run into problems.

The computer industry is currently going through the "clone wars" in which a number of competitors have been turning out equipment virtually identical to the IBM personal computer. By definition, a clone is a near-identical copy, while a compatible is a machine that will run the same software that an IBM will run. Combined sales of a wide number of nationally-distributed brands and a few "who the heck are they" brands have actually surpassed the sales of the IBM PC. All of this competition has resulted in price-cutting by IBM as well, so finding a deal on equipment that meets your family's needs should not be a problem. The only worry is whether you'll get a machine that will perform according to the claims of its manufacturer and that has replacement parts readily available. Always try to talk to someone who has used a clone before you decide to buy one. It's also a good idea to research the particular manufacturer and machine through current periodicals that review equipment. Expect discounting and shop around for the best deal.

The cellular car telephone is a status symbol to many Americans, another technological example of one-up-manship. More than a few people chatting into a handset as they drive down the expressway seem as concerned that other motorists see them using that status symbol as they are in conducting business. Unless you spend a considerable portion of your workweek in your car and can actually profit from using your drive time by making and receiving calls, it's probably not worth the cost.

"The car phone is important to me because I can call my next stop-off in advance and avoid making unnecessary trips or looking for pay phones," explained a salesman. A television investigative reporter uses the 45-minute trip in from the suburbs as a time to set up all of his interviews for the day. Cellular telephoning divides a metropolitan area into segments called cells which handle hundreds of conversations at the same time. A transmitter at the cell site sends your signal to a center that does computerized switching to the local telephone network. This eliminates the static and fadeouts of conventional mobile telephones.

Finding a bargain in a cellular phone requires some research on pricing and likely billings. There will be several competing carriers in your area that charge a flat fee for access to their system and a usage charge for each minute of conversation logged. Compare various pricing plans based upon what you'll likely use and what geographic areas you most frequently travel. Call-waiting and call-holding are other features available. When you're selecting the equipment to be put in your car, investigate the track record of the manufacturer. Pick one that will likely be around for the long haul. You can either buy or lease equipment. Some companies offer special equipment deals for becoming a customer, though you can probably expect to pay less than $1,000 for a basic model and a $50 monthly service charge that doesn't include individual calls. A number of companies also permit use of your system in a different geographic area through special arrangement. Installation is important, since an inexperienced installer can negate all the good research you've done by doing a bad job that results in interference or generally poor reception.

Shopping at home is another modern concept that has taken off. The successful launching of Home Shopping Network did more than produce an explosively successful new stock issue on Wall Street. HSN ties together retailing and broadcasting in its cable television format that features hosts hawking everything from fur coats to cookware. The company grew from $900,000 in annual sales to estimated revenues of $150 million for 1986. HSN produces two live programs devoted to touting merchandise for sale. Transmitted by satellite, the programs run 24 hours a day, seven days a week. Other competitors are offering such services as well. Customers watch the show, pick an item they like and then telephone an "800" number shown on their television screen. After some basic questions regarding the buyer and order are asked, the item will be dispatched from a warehouse to be processed and shipped by United Parcel Service within two days. Amid a trend to discount chains, direct marketing and busy Americans with less time to spend looking for items, shopping at home is expected to continue its rapid growth. But even this thoroughly modern idea requires some careful handling, since it is based on the concept of impulse buying run amuck. A real shopping junkie can get into serious trouble with unnecessary orders unless there is careful consideration of costs and needs beforehand.

Opening one's own business is a concept that has been around since capitalism got its start, yet it has become a decidedly modern fad in recent years. More and more Americans beaten down by modern corporate life are saying goodbye to their jobs and investing their time and money in a business of their own. It's a sweet dream that works out fine for many of them. Unfortunately, starting up a business has never been more arduous than today, with eight out of 10 new firms failing within five years.

Figuring out "what's hot" or "what's not" sometimes dictates success or failure. Greatest growth lately has been in computer firms and radio-television stores, while incorporations of real estate and insurance businesses have plunged. Yet what makes or breaks any new venture has far more to do with how carefully you've researched it, how well you've financed it and how competent you are at doing daily bookkeeping. "People try too soon and they hardly last any time at all," said Dagny DuVal, who with husband Tim owns Plant Specialists Inc., a successful indoor and outdoor landscaping firm in Queens, N.Y. "They also don't realize that you have to live, breathe and sleep the firm." In a typical family effort, Dagny does administrative work and Tim handles sales and design for the company, which has grown to 65 employees in 13 years.

Currently, less than 10 percent of the nation's small business owners are women, though the percentage is growing. "A lot of women in middle management decide to leave the corporate world to become consultants, for example," said Judi Schindler, who started up Schindler Public Relations in Chicago eight years ago. "In other cases, women in, say, health care or social work may not have the usual qualifications for positions at big companies, so they decide to start their own interesting businesses."

Since many new businesses go bankrupt simply because they never had enough money, it is vitally important to do your homework. First of all, work up a detailed list of all expenses required for your proposed venture, such as the building, equipment, supplies, vehicles, salaries and cash flow needs. Figure in additional costs that may fluctuate, such as overtime salaries or equipment used during peak periods. To get started, you need at least enough money for six months of expenses, based on solid financial information that permits you to monitor your progress. Most important, know how much income you'll pull in and how much you're likely to keep as profit. Estimate overall losses and whatever tax writeoffs may be incurred in getting things going, as well as how much money you'll need in reserve for emergencies. Formulate a detailed balance sheet for operation of the entire business. Make sure you've selected a business worthy of your effort, not just something that seems intriguing. Define your product or service carefully so that a second party, such as a bank, can understand exactly what you're planning to do. Provide a well-researched feasibility study that indicates the profile of the consumer you're aiming at and the likelihood of that consumer paying the price you ask.

The Small Business Administration will guarantee 85 percent of a bank loan to a small business, or $500,000. Expect plenty of paperwork, however. Some banks have preferred lender status and can commit a large portion of the SBA guarantee without applying directly to the agency. Many new businesses are started up with money from relatives and friends, while others take on permanent financial partners. There are countless loan arrangements, such as those strictly for supplies, inventory or season periods. But in all cases, no one is likely to shell out money unless you have your act together on paper and give solid evidence that you're destined to succeed.

Tax laws are having plenty of effect on professionals. Many closely-held businesses may be more profitable if organized as partnerships instead of corporations. The minimum tax rate on corporations is now raised to 20 percent from 15 percent and more items are included in computing the tax. At the same time, the tax rate for an individual could be lower than the top corporate rate, which falls to 34 percent from 46 percent. A partnership pays no tax and the partners declare their share of any gains or losses on their individual tax returns. However, incorporation still has some advantages, such as the chance to borrow from retirement plans, so it is important for the individual businessman to carefully compute all of the options.

The S corporation is an increasingly popular alternative which has elements of a corporation and a partnership. S corporations generally do not pay corporate income taxes, but instead pass through to their shareholders income, deductions, losses and other items, and their tax attributes. The S corporation is not subject to the strict corporate alternative minimum tax applicable to regular corporations. To elect to become an S corporation, there must be 35 shareholders or fewer, except that a married couple filing a joint return is counted as one shareholder. There is one class of stock only, though different voting rights are permitted for different shares of stock. Generally, there is no limit on the type of business that may be conducted by an S corporation, except that financial institutions and insurance companies are generally not permitted to be S corporations. Capital gains realized by S corporations are taxed to their shareholders at ordinary income rates, so individual tax brackets are the critical factor. New and existing S corporations and partnerships will be required to use calendar tax years as their fiscal year, thereby eliminating an opportunity for owners to defer tax. Stockholders are taxed directly as in a partnership so that business losses offset family income, but shareholders also benefit from the limited financial liability of a corporation.

Deregulation is a modern idea that is getting mixed reviews, particularly in regard to the airline industry.

It is true that many air fares are lower. But the number of different types of discount fares is mind-boggling, many times requiring 30-day advance reservations and a penalty for cancellation. In addition, a number of airlines have been failing or merging under duress, unable to survive cutthroat competition. Airline mergers generally mean increased fares and fewer flights, although discounts are still offered and the high costs are tossed to business travelers and others who are unable to make plans far in advance.

These days, it is truly important to plan trips in advance. Even a one-week advance reservation can sometimes mean significant savings. A typical round-trip fare may go for $190 if booked four weeks in advance, increasing to $260 with two-weeks notice and perhaps reaching $500 if done on short notice. There frequently are restrictions on days that one leaves and what days one must stay over. This is easiest for senior citizens or those with routine travel demands, yet it undeniably does cut costs. Business travel in particular makes it worth doing your homework. Airlines definitely take this into account in their fare strategies. A little advance planning and organization can make a difference. In addition, there are a number of senior citizens flight programs that permit extensive annual travel at set discount rates, perfect for those who visit relatives in other parts of the country regularly.

Frequent flier programs, which offer free flights or discounted flights after enough mileage points have been accumulated, are also worth considering by travelers. Airlines have stepped up efforts to use them as a special lure. Some offer quadruple bonus mileage points these days on certain routes. Other carriers have linked their frequent flier programs so that points are accumulated by flying on more than one airline. Some are even more inventive. For example, Midway Airlines of Chicago gives passengers who make 60 roundtrips anywhere $2,500 in credit in a Citicorp Diners Club account or $2,000 in Citicorp traveler's checks. While frequent flier programs inevitably mean some travelers will take some trips solely to build mileage toward free or discounted flights, they are nonetheless a worthwhile option in the confusingly modern world of air travel. If you're vacation traveling, keep in mind that some excursion deals may sometimes have late passenger cancellations or fail to fill their quota of passengers. If you're flexible and let your travel agent know you're willing to leave on fairly short notice, you might get an excellent last-minute deal.

Modern ideas aren't so difficult to deal with if you're careful to make the right moves. It is important to keep in mind, however, that many ideas ranging from four-channel stereophonic sound to the Edsel have turned out bad. Your common sense will determine whether the rest of the 1980s will be costly to your family or a time of setting up the right framework to make money.

15   Your Tax Questions

Ever ask a vendor on a street corner where a certain address is, or a store clerk where the restrooms are, and receive a truly pained look before begrudgingly being given an answer to your query? "Guess they've been asked that question before," you might say to yourself.

It seems a lot of questions do come up again and again in life. Each month in Playboy Magazine, for example, the "Playboy Adviser" column answers questions about what are supposedly wide-ranging topics. But, if you took out some of the recurring questions about sex and stereos, there frankly wouldn't be a whole lot left.

And so it goes with the new tax laws. Whether at cocktail parties, a football game or coffee at the office, it seems some folks are asking the same questions over and over again. "I keep telling them that, no, the IRA isn't dead and, no, not everyone's tax bracket will be as low as 28 percent, so much that I feel like a broken record," said one frustrated tax accountant. "And you know, it doesn't get any better."

To make things better for you or to give you a good shot at being a know-it-all at your next cocktail party, the following are some of the most-asked questions about the new tax laws.

Q. In 1983, I set up a Clifford trust with $30,000 of cash and designated my four-year-old son as beneficiary. During 1984 through 1986, the income earned by the trust and distributed to my son has been reported on my son's tax return and the appropriate taxes paid. Does the new tax bill affect the taxes paid by my son?

A. Yes, your toddler's brief respite from the full force of the IRS has drawn to a close. The unearned income of children under age 14 will be taxed to the child at the parent's rate. However, the tax rules do allow the first $1,000 of unearned income to be taxed at the child's rate. The actual computations for the child's taxes will be somewhat complex, because it will require the simultaneous preparation of the child's and the parent's tax returns. The fact that the Clifford trust was set up earlier has no bearing on the taxability of the amount.

Q. I thought the tax rate reduction to 28 percent would be effective for 1988 and beyond, but my neighbor says it is possible for me to be taxed at a 33 percent rate. Is this true?

A. Yes, and you are not alone in misunderstanding this. It is important that you found out sooner, rather than later. After 1987, couples filing a joint return will pay 15 percent on the first $29,750 of taxable income and 28 percent of any income above that amount. For single taxpayers, the 28 percent rate starts at $17,850 and for heads of household, the 28 percent starts at $23,900. However, the 15 percent rate is phased out for joint returns with taxable income between $71,900 and $149,250, and for singles with taxable income between $43,150 and $89,560.

The benefit is phased out by adding a 5 percent tax on income above the bottom of these ranges. So, for income in the phase-out range, the marginal tax rate will increase to 33 percent.

Q. My wife and I both work and in prior years have been able to deduct 10 percent of the lesser of $30,000 or the earned

income of whichever of our incomes was lower. Is this now kaput?

A.   Yes, kaput is right. The two-earner deduction, which intended to help redress the "marriage tax penalty" imposed on two income couples, has been repealed for tax years after 1986.

Q.   In prior years, I was able to pay less income tax by income averaging. It meant a lot because I've had a lot of promotions. Will I still be able to income average in the future?

A.   Go ahead and enjoy your success, but be willing to pay for it year-by-year. Income-averaging is repealed for tax years beginning in 1987.

Q.   For the last several years, my wife and I have each contributed $2,000 to our IRA. What exactly are the new rules?

A.   It depends on your situation. If neither you nor your spouse is covered by a qualified retirement plan, you may continue to contribute and deduct up to $2,000 per earner to an IRA or $2,250 to a spousal IRA if only one spouse is employed. But if *either* you or your spouse is covered by one of these plans, your annual IRA deduction will phase out between certain levels of adjusted gross income. For most people, the loss or reduction of the IRA deduction will certainly be missed.

Q.   What does it mean to be a member of a qualified plan in terms of IRA deductibility?

A.   The term "qualified retirement plan" includes any of the normal retirement plans, such as pension plan, profit-sharing plan or employee stock ownership plan, in which the employee is an active participant. The worker must have met the eligibility requirements and, generally speaking, be entitled to receive benefits under the provisions of the plan. Even if an employee's benefits are not fully vested, or not vested at all, he or she usually is still considered an active participant.

Q. I'm self-employed. Can I continue contributing 20 percent of my self-employment income to my money-purchase Keogh plan?
A. Contributions to Keogh plans remain basically unchanged. A self-employed individual in a money-purchase Keogh plan can continue to contribute up to 20 percent of his or her net self-employment income and will be allowed a current deduction. Keep in mind that such plans must be established before the end of the taxable year in which a deduction is to be claimed.

Q. Even though the contribution I make to an IRA is no longer tax-deductible, is there any benefit to continuing IRA contributions?
A. You bet. Individuals ineligible for a tax-deductible contribution to an IRA can continue to benefit from the tax-free accumulation of earnings on contributions of up to $2,000 per year. Investment set aside in the IRA compound at a faster rate than taxable investments because of the deferral of the taxes on the earnings. However, before making nondeductible IRA contributions, an individual should compare other types of tax-deferred or tax-free investments such as municipal bonds or annuities. Also, be aware that when you withdraw funds from a nondeductible IRA, a pro rata portion of the dollars withdrawn will be deemed attributable to earnings and be subject to taxation, and even to penalty, if you are under age 59½.

Q. I am confused about the phaseout of the consumer interest deduction and wonder if it is more beneficial to borrow money sooner, rather than in future years.
A. While the tax law's goal is that all consumer interest such as interest on credit cards and car loans will no longer be deductible, this provision is phased in over four years. In 1987, 65 percent of consumer interest paid during the year is allowed as an itemized deduction, in 1988 it declines to 40 percent, then it slides in 1989 to 20 percent and in 1990 falls to

10 percent. It disappears as a deduction in 1991. The new law focuses on the concept of interest paid, and does not concern itself with the date on which the money that generates the interest expense was borrowed. Therefore, all consumer interest paid in 1987 and beyond, regardless of when the loan was obtained, will be subject to the interest limitations. It makes good sense not to be paying significant loan interest beyond 1988.

Q. In the past, tax return preparation fees were deductible as an itemized deduction on Schedule A of IRS Form 1040. In addition, other miscellaneous items such as investment expenses and union dues were also deductible as itemized deductions. Will these types of items continue to be deductible in the future?
A. Miscellaneous deductions will continue to be tax-deductible items in future years. But there's a catch. The amount of such deductions will be subject to a new limitation. All such miscellaneous deductions will be pulled together, and a tax deduction will be allowed for the excess of this amount over 2 percent of the taxpayer's adjusted gross income. This will effectively eliminate this tax deduction for the majority of taxpayers, unless they have an unusually large amount of miscellaneous deductions compared to their income level.

Q. In 1986, we took the full amount of our charitable contributions made during the year as a deduction even though we did not itemize. Will this deduction continue in the future?
A. Those who do not itemize will no longer be able to deduct charitable contributions. Those who do itemize, however, will be able to deduct them.

Q. I am a limited partner in a real estate partnership. In 1986, I had a loss from this activity which I used to offset other income. How does the new tax law affect my investment?

A. You will not spell relief "T-A-X R-E-F-O-R-M." The new law severely limits the ability of so-called tax-shelter losses to offset income from business and investment activities. For individuals, estates, trusts, personal service corporations and certain closely-held corporations, there are limits on deductible losses from passive activities. Taxpayers affected will separate their income and losses into three categories, or "baskets."

The first basket will consist of wages and active trade or business income. The second will be portfolio income, such as interest and dividends. The third will include all "passive" activities, which are defined as activities in which the taxpayer does not materially participate, including rental activities. A limited partnership is always considered passive. Material participation essentially means daily activity. Under the new rules, passive losses and credits can only offset passive income. This provision is effective for losses or credits in tax years beginning after 1986, arising from investments made after Oct. 22, 1986.

A special transition rule phasing in the disallowance of passive losses is allowed for interests purchased prior to Oct. 22, 1986. Under the phase-in, 65 percent of passive losses are allowed against nonpassive income in 1987, 40 percent in 1988, 20 percent in 1989 and 10 percent in 1990. So, if your investment was purchased prior to enactment and generated a $50,000 loss in 1987, $32,500 of this loss would be allowed as an offset to nonpassive income, with the remaining $17,500 able to offset only passive income.

Q. The three-unit apartment building which I own generates losses of approximately $15,000 per year. Under the new passive loss rules, will this amount continue to be deductible, or will I lose the deduction?
A. Generally speaking, after the phase-out period, passive losses will only be allowed to the extent of passive income. Rental activities, by definition, will be deemed to be passive losses and the amount would not be deductible.

There is, however, a provision allowing $25,000 of passive rental losses from activities in which the taxpayer actively participates in the management of the property. Active participation means overall management and leasing activity. However, any disallowed losses are carried to future years or until the property is sold. The $25,000 limitation for deducting these losses is phased out at the rate of 50 cents on the dollar for taxpayers with adjusted gross income in excess of $100,000. As a result, losses under this provision are no longer available for taxpayers with adjusted gross income in excess of $150,000.

Q. Within my investment portfolio, I have many stocks which have substantially increased in value since their purchase. How will the tax law change affect the taxes associated with such gains if I sell?
A. These taxes will probably rise. Effective in 1987, the favorable tax treatment afforded long-term capital gains will no longer exist. Rather than the 20 percent maximum capital gains rate of the past, the maximum for 1987 is 28 percent. From then on, the gains are taxed as ordinary income at the taxpayer's marginal rate.

Q. In the past, I was able to sell stock at year end and reflect the gain in the following tax year when the sale was settled. This effectively allowed deferral of the taxes on the gain. Can I still do this?
A. No. The provisions for this type of deferral are repealed. The entire gain will be recorded in the year in which the trade of the security occurs, thus accelerating the amount of tax due on the transaction.

16   Winners and Losers and Help Sources

Top 10 stock funds over the past five years

1) Fidelity Magellan Fund   up 297.99%
   Load fund, Fidelity Investments
   Boston, Mass.

2) BBK International Fund   up 273.91%
   No-load fund, Bailard, Biehl &
     Kaiser
   San Mateo, Calif.
   ($10,000 minimum)

3) Merrill Lynch Pacific Fund   up 273.43%
   Load, Merrill Lynch & Co.
   New York, N.Y.

4) Vanguard World-International   up 261.48%
     Growth Portfolio
   No-load, Vanguard Group
   Valley Forge, Pa.

5) Fidelity Select-Health Care   up 243.57%
   Load, Fidelity Investments
   Boston, Mass.

6) Oppenheimer Target Fund   up 235.42%
   Load, Oppenheimer Management
      Corp.
   New York, N.Y.

7) Phoenix Growth Fund   up 233.15%
   Load, Phoenix Investment Counsel
      Inc.
   Hartford, Conn.

8) Quest for Value Fund   up 227.83%
   No-load, Oppenheimer Capital
      Corp.
   New York, N.Y.

9) Putnam International Equities   up 226.96%
   Load, Putnam Management Co.
   Boston, Mass.

10) Evergreen Total Return Fund   up 220.76%
    No-load, Saxon Woods Asset
       Management Corp.
    Harrison, N.Y.

Data was compiled by Lipper Analytical Services for the period 9/30/81 through 9/30/86. Only funds still open to investors are included.

Worst-performing stock mutual funds over the past five years

1) 44 Wall Street Fund	down 64.27%
2) First Investors Natural Resources	down 38.64%
3) American Heritage Fund	down 27.63%
4) Steadman Oceanographic, Technology & Growth Fund	down 23.88%
5) Interstate Capital Growth Fund	down 21.86%

Data compiled by Lipper Analytical Services.

Investment letters

The following investment letters were mentioned or quoted in this book:

Closed-End Fund Monthly
  Update
7800 Red Rd.
South Miami, Fla. 33143
(305) 665-6500

Growth Stock Outlook
P.O. Box 15381
Chevy Chase, Md. 20815
(301) 654-5205

Dines Letter
P.O. Box 22
Belvedere, Calif. 94920
(415) 435-5458

Hulbert Financial Digest
643 S. Carolina Ave. S.E.,
Washington, D.C. 20003
(800) 443-0100 Ext. 459

Managed Account Reports
5513 Twin Knolls
Columbia, Md. 21045
(301) 730-5365

Mutual Fund Strategist
P.O. Box 466
Burlington, Vt. 05402
(802) 658-3513

New Issues
3471 N. Federal Hwy.
Ft. Lauderdale, Fla. 33306
(800) 327-6720

Norwood Index
6134 N. Milwaukee Ave.
Chicago, Ill. 60646
(312) 763-1540

100 Highest Yields
860 Federal Hwy. One
North Palm Beach, Fla.
33408-3825
(800) 327-7717

Prudent Speculator
P.O. Box 1767
Santa Monica, Calif. 90406
(213) 395-5275

Stockmarket Cycles
2260 Cahuenga Blvd.
Los Angeles, Calif. 90068
(800) 528-6600 Ext. 237

Value Line OTC Special
  Situations
711 Third Ave.
New York, N.Y. 10017
(212) 687-3965

Weekly Takeover Target
  Forecast
5290 Overpass Rd.
Santa Barbara, Calif. 93111
(805) 964-7841

Zweig Forecast
900 Third Ave.
New York, N.Y. 10022
(212) 644-0040

Investment firms

The following are investment firms whose products are mentioned in this book:

Alliance Capital Management
  Corp.
140 Broadway
New York, N.Y. 10005
(800) 221-5672

American Capital Funds
2800 Post Oak Blvd.
Houston, Tex. 77056
(800) 231-3638

Calvert Group
1700 Pennsylvania Ave., N.W.
Washington, D.C. 20006
(800) 368-2748

Christopher M. Funk & Co.
111 N. Fourth St.
Lafayette, Ind. 47902
(317) 423-2644

Colorado Commodities
   Management
345 St. Peter St.
St. Paul, Minn. 55102
(612) 224-2744

Commonwealth Group
P.O. Box 8687
Richmond, Va. 23226
(800) 527-9500

Dean Witter Reynolds
One World Trade Center
59th Floor
New York, N.Y. 10048
(800) 222-3326

Desai & Co.
444 Castro St., Suite 917
Mountain View, Calif. 94041
(415) 964-5760

Dreyfus Corp.
767 Fifth Ave.
New York, N.Y. 10153
(800) 645-6561

Evergreen Funds
550 Mamaroneck Ave.
Harrison, N.Y. 10528
(800) 635-0003

Fidelity Investments
82 Devonshire St.
Boston, Mass. 02109
(800) 544-6666

Financial Programs
P.O. Box 2040
Denver, Colo. 80201
(800) 525-8085

First Investors Management
   Co.
120 Wall St.
New York, N.Y. 10005
(800) 423-4026

GT Global Funds
601 Montgomery St.
Suite 1400
San Francisco, Calif. 94111
(800) 824-1580

E. F. Hutton Group Inc.
One Battery Park Plaza
New York, N.Y. 10004
(212) 742-5000

IDS Financial Services
1000 Roanoke Building
Minneapolis, Minn. 55474
(800) 328-8300

Kemper Financial Services
120 S. LaSalle St.
Chicago, Ill. 60603
(800) 621-1148

R. Meeder & Assoc.
6000 Memorial Dr.
Dublin, Ohio 43017
(614) 766-7000

Merrill Lynch & Co. Funds
P.O. Box 9011
Princeton, N.J. 08540
(800) 262-4636

New Alternatives Fund
295 Northern Blvd.
Great Neck, N.Y. 11021
(516) 466-0808

New England Life Funds
501 Boylston St.
Boston, Mass. 02117
(800) 343-7104

John Nuveen & Co.
333 W. Wacker Dr.
Chicago, Ill. 60606
(800) 621-2431

Oppenheimer Management
  Corp.
Two Broadway
New York, N.Y. 10004
(800) 525-7048

PaineWebber Inc.
1285 Avenue of the Americas
New York, N.Y. 10019
(212) 713-2000

Parnassus Fund
244 California St.
San Francisco, Calif. 94111
(415) 392-5595

Pax World
224 State St.
Portsmouth, N.H. 03801
(603) 431-8022

Phoenix Investment Counsel
  Inc.
One American Row
Hartford, Conn. 06115
(800) 243-1574

Pioneer Group
60 State St.
Boston, Mass. 02109
(800) 225-6292

Putnam Financial Services
One Post Office Sq.
Boston, Mass. 02109
(800) 225-2465

Salomon Brothers Inc.
One New York Plaza
New York, N.Y. 10004
(212) 747-7000

Securities Investors
  International
150 E. 58th St., 28th Floor
New York, N.Y. 10155
(212) 980-9412

Shearson Lehman Brothers
  Inc.
World Financial Center
New York, N.Y. 10285
(212) 298-2000

Stein Roe & Farnham
P.O. Box 1143
Chicago, Ill. 60690
(800) 621-0320

Strong Funds
815 E. Mason St.
Milwaukee, Wis. 53202
(800) 368-3863

T. Rowe Price
100 E. Pratt St.
Baltimore, Md. 21202
(800) 638-5660

Tucker Anthony Funds
Three Center Plaza
Boston, Mass. 02108
(800) 225-6258

Twentieth Century Investors
P.O. Box 200
Kansas City, Mo. 64141
(816) 531-5575

USAA Investment
  Management Co.
USAA Building
San Antonio, Tex. 78288
(800) 531-8181

U.S. Trust Co.
45 Wall St.
New York, N.Y. 10005
(212) 806-4500

Value Line Securities
711 Third Ave.
New York, N.Y. 10017
(800) 223-0818

Vanguard Group
P.O. Box 2600
Valley Forge, Pa. 19482
(800) 662-7447

Van Kampen Merritt Inc.
1901 N. Naper Blvd.
Naperville, Ill. 60566
(312) 369-8880

Index

A

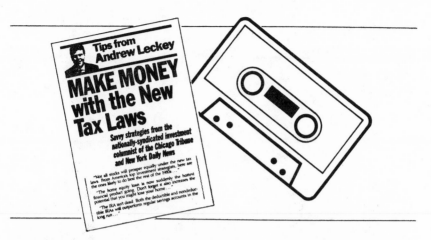